CH00925551

THE MERCHANT NAVY SEAMAN

POCKET MANUAL 1939–1945

THE MERCHANT NAVY SEAMAN

POCKET MANUAL 1939–1945

Edited by Chris McNab

CASEMATE

Oxford & Philadelphia

Published in Great Britain and
the United States of America in 2018 by
CASEMATE PUBLISHERS
The Old Music Hall, 106–108 Cowley Road, Oxford OX4 1JE, UK
1950 Lawrence Road, Havertown, PA 19083, USA

Introduction and chapter introductory texts by Chris McNab
© Casemate Publishers 2018

Hardback Edition: ISBN 978-1-61200-657-4
Digital Edition: ISBN 978-1-61200-658-1

A CIP record for this book is available from the British Library

Printed in the United Kingdom by TJ International

The information and advice contained in the documents in this book is solely for
historical interest and does not constitute advice. The publisher accepts no liability for the
consequences of following any of the advice in this book.

For a complete list of Casemate titles, please contact:

CASEMATE PUBLISHERS (UK)
Telephone (01865) 241249
Fax (01865) 794449
Email: casemate-uk@casematepublishers.co.uk
www.casematepublishers.co.uk

CASEMATE PUBLISHERS (US)
Telephone (610) 853-9131
Fax (610) 853-9146
Email: casemate@casematepublishers.com
www.casematepublishers.com

Cover design by Katie Gabriel Allen

CONTENTS

INTRODUCTION

On 12 September 1939, scarcely a week after the German invasion of Poland and the onset of hostilities between Germany and Britain, the British king, George VI, issued a message via the nation's newspapers. It addressed a very specific group of people, who although they did not serve in the armed forces were nonetheless utterly central to the survival of the United Kingdom in the expanding conflict:

> In these anxious days I would like to express to all Officers and Men and in The British Merchant Navy and The British Fishing Fleets my confidence in their unfailing determination to play their vital part in defence. To each one I would say: Yours is a task no less essential to my people's experience than that allotted to the Navy, Army and Air Force. Upon you the Nation depends for much of its foodstuffs and raw materials and for the transport of its troops overseas. You have a long and glorious history, and I am proud to bear the title 'Master of the Merchant Navy and Fishing Fleets'. I know that you will carry out your duties with resolution and with fortitude, and that high chivalrous traditions of your calling are safe in your hands. God keep you and prosper you in your great task.

George VI knew, and was doubtless reminded by his government advisors, that to a large degree the future victory or defeat of Britain lay in the hands on its non-combatant merchant fleet. As an island nation, Britain was disproportionately reliant upon maritime imports. All of its oil, now vital for keeping the wheels of war industry running, was shipped in from abroad, as was 54 per cent of its iron ore, 93 per cent of its lead and 95 per cent of its zinc. On the domestic side, some 70 per cent of food was imported, including 91 per cent of the country's butter, 70 per cent of its cereals and fats, 50 per cent of its meat and 80 per cent of its fruits. It was apparent to all, especially in light of the punishing experience of the U-boat campaign during the previous world war, that the greatest threat to Britain's sustained resistance to Nazi Germany was the severing of its Merchant Navy lifelines.

Eclectic Service

The Merchant Navy, as it was known by the onset of World War II, should not be regarded as a holistic entity, like the Royal Navy. In reality, the term was essentially a convenient conceptual label, bestowed by King George V following World War I, for what was actually a swarming mass of independent and physically diverse commercial shipping. Under the title 'Merchant Navy', therefore, fell a typology of vessels in which the only unifying factor appeared to be that they all floated on water. They included (based on the 1940 publication *His Majesty's Merchant Navy*): ocean-going liners, intermediate liners, cargo liners, refrigerated ships, fruit ships, cargo ships (themselves of numerous types), colliers, tankers, whale-oil ships, cross-channel packets, continental and Thames excursion steamers, paddle steamers, timber carriers, coastal ships, short sea traders, cable ships, tugs, ferries, harbor craft, canal craft, ore carriers, river boats, cruising ships, hospital ships, troopships and fishing vessels. The men and, more rarely, women who served aboard these vessels were as contrasting as the ships themselves, ranging from university-educated officers to ship's boys from rough parts of industrial Britain. In November 1939, the writer Montague Smith described the archetypal British merchant sailor in the *Daily Mail*: 'He is usually dressed rather like a tramp. His sweater is worn, his trousers frayed, while what was once a cap is perched askew on his tanned face. He wears no gold braid or gold buttons: neither does he jump to the salute briskly. Nobody goes out of his way to call him a 'hero', or pin medals on his breast. No–he is just a seaman of the British Merchant Service. Yet he serves in our Front Line today.'

Despite its often ragged appearance, the Merchant Navy carried with it international prestige. It was the world's largest merchant marine. In 1938 it had more than 192,000 personnel, including 50,700 Chinese and Indian sailors. Yet if Britain was to sustain the war effort, many more sailors and more boats would be required. Finding the right levels of manpower was at first problematic, because merchant sailors were, to all intents and purposes, casual, non-military labour. At the outbreak of war, the sailors were given the option of switching to less hazardous land-based careers, or joining the armed forces, but those who decided to stay in the service still labored from contract to contract, unpaid when work dried up.

Desperate Times

This situation produced some evident absurdities. For example, if a sailor's ship was attacked and sunk, the moment the ship slipped under the waves the sailor (if he survived) was no longer paid. Such commercial heartlessness was given real substance by the terrible losses already being suffered by the Merchant Navy at the hands of German aircraft, mines and, above all, U-boats. The first ship sunk by the Germans was the transatlantic passenger liner *Athenia*, destroyed on 3 September 1939 by *U-30* 370km (229 miles) north-west of the northern tip of Ireland. But by the end of that month, another 51 vessels had been destroyed, and by the end of the year, a total of 165 ships had been downed.

Far worse was to come the following year. The German conquest of Western Europe meant that France's Atlantic ports fell under Kriegsmarine control. U-boats could now sail easily and directly into the British Atlantic sea lanes. Further campaigns were launched in the Mediterranean, although the U-boat threat there was limited by the narrow and British-controlled entrance to the Mediterranean at the Straits of Gibraltar. (This didn't stop the Merchant Navy in the Mediterranean being harried by German and Italian maritime aircraft and surface vessels.) Both the increasing numbers of U-boats and the improving German 'Wolf Pack' tactics inflicted hideous losses on the ships and sailors – 1,059 vessels in 1940 rising to 1,299 in 1941.

There was some temporary relief in the Atlantic when Hitler's invasion of the Soviet Union in June 1941 drew away attention momentarily away from the West. Yet that action in itself opened up a new front in the Merchant Navy war as, from August 1941, Britain began to make maritime supply runs through the Arctic waters to northern Russia. These journeys have become infamous as trials of sheer human endurance and perfect misery. The round-trip journeys were some 4,000km (2,500 miles) in distance, and for much of that journey the shipping would have been under horrific repetitive air and sea attacks. Added to the sailors' burdens were the sub-zero conditions experienced north of the Arctic Circle, which locked every surface in tons of ice (some ships might be carrying 150 tons of extra weight by the time they reached port), and the mighty storms. About one out of every 20 ships that attempted the passage would not survive.

At least the levels of threat encountered by the Merchant Navy sorted out some anomalies in Merchant Navy service. The 'Emergency Work (Merchant Navy) Order, Notice No. M198', issued in May 1941, organized all merchant seamen into a Merchant Navy Reserve Pool. Every sailor, and 60,000 ex-mariners, were obliged to put their names onto the register, and the government could assign their manpower to whichever vessel needed it. Furthermore, merchant sailors were now obliged to give service for the duration of the conflict. In return, it was agreed that they would receive a wage for the entire war, including any time they spent as prisoner, plus they received two days' paid leave for each month served.

Merchant Shipping and Escorts

For Britain, the great danger of the U-boat threat in particular was that, at times, sinkings exceeded the rates at which ships could be built, even with Britain's historically formidable powers of shipbuilding. Winston Churchill famously said later in his life that 'the only thing that ever frightened me during the war was the U-boat threat', and did so with good reason. Some of the losses were counterbalanced by the output of British dockyards, plus the increasing contributions of Commonwealth allies, particularly Canada. But in 1940 and 1941 the losses were far in excess of the commissions.

What really helped correct the balance was the entry of the United States into the war in December 1941 (see below). This event brought into play the vast and expanding industrial resources of the United States, particularly via its Emergency Shipbuilding Program, which actually began in January 1941, before the USA entered direct hostilities. This programme was notable for the unstoppable output of 'Liberty' ships, low-cost cargo vessels designed specifically for mass production. In total, 18 US shipyards built 2,710 Liberty ships between 1941 and 1945. To this total we should also add the 531 faster, more modern 'Victory' ships built between 1944 and the end of the war. In one record-breaking effort, a Liberty ship was produced from keel-laying to launch in under five days. Such powerhouse levels of production meant that the Allies would permanently escape the scarcity of merchant ships, especially once efforts in the wider war brought victories in the fight against the U-boats.

Although the British focus of this book is on the Merchant Navy, their efforts went hand-in-hand with the escort duties provided by the Royal Navy, Commonwealth fleets and eventually the US Navy. At the very beginning of the war, the convoy system that had proved so successful in World War I was immediately reinstated. These convoys numbered initially about 30–40 vessels, but even this sizeable number of vessels was protected at first by just one or two Royal Navy warships, typically ageing destroyers, frigates or corvettes. The defensive capability of the convoys was boosted by the Defensively Equipped Merchant Ships (DEMS). As their name implies, the DEMS were merchant vessels equipped with basic armament, mainly anti-aircraft machine guns and automatic cannon and various surplus low-angle (LA) or high-angle (HA) guns. The guns were manned by men of the Royal Navy and the Royal Artillery Maritime Regiment, although some 150,000 civilian sailors were also trained in gun support and operation.

A major step forward in the escort capability of the British came with the introduction of the Lend-Lease Program, in which the United States lent its British and other anti-Nazi states military materiel – including warships – in return for no-cost leases on army and naval bases in Allied territory. In September 1940, the US Navy provided the British with some 50 destroyers which – although many were of obsolete types – once appropriately fitted out with anti-submarine weaponry provided an encouraging boost to British escort power. Alongside this programme, the UK also had its own indigenous shipbuilding effort, focused especially on producing corvettes and destroyers equipped with anti-aircraft and anti-submarine weaponry, including depth charges and, later, the 'Hedgehog' A/S mortar. These weapons, combined with increasingly sophisticated detection equipment such as ASDIC, the High Frequency Radio Detection Finder (Huff-Duff) and centimetric radar, made life more dangerous for the U-boats and safer for the Merchant Navy.

Enter the United States

One of the pivotal points in the Atlantic War against the U-boats was the entry of the United States into the war as an official combatant in December 1941. The United States had, in fact, been sliding into such status for some months before the Japanese attack on Pearl Harbor on 7 December 1941, and the subsequent and wildly inadvisable German declaration of war against America four days later. It had lost both merchant and military vessels to German actions before the December, hence was already on a semi-war footing.

The US equivalent of the British Merchant Navy was the US Merchant Marine. In the inter-war years, the Merchant Marine had experienced a decline in fortunes. There had been limited investment in merchant shipbuilding and renovation, meaning that its 1,340 pre-war vessels were often ageing or obsolete. The total manpower of the Merchant Marine in 1940 was just 55,000 men, roughly the same number as foreign sailors employed by the British Merchant Navy. From the mid-1930s, with war on the horizon in Europe, the US government had already recognised that the Merchant Marine needed augmentation in both manpower and shipping. An important step forward was the Merchant Marine Act of 1936, signed into being by President Franklin D. Roosevelt. Through its numerous statutes, this Act galvanised shipbuilding while also professionalising the way merchant ship service operated. A key statement of the Act was that 'The United States shall have a merchant marine … [to] serve as a naval or military auxiliary in time of war or national emergency … [and] should be operated by highly trained and efficient citizens of the United States and that the United States Navy and the Merchant Marine of the United States should work closely together to promote the maximum integration of the total seapower forces of the United States. . .' The Act also led, in 1938, to the establishment of the US Maritime Service, whose purpose it was to train the next generations of officers and men for service in the Merchant Marine. Under the jurisdiction, variously, of the US Maritime Commission and the US Coast Guard (the ranks, grades and ratings for Maritime Service personnel were the same as those in the Coast Guard), the Maritime Service developed a chain of basic and advanced training bases across the United States between 1939 and 1943. Not only did these facilities upskill men for the Merchant Marine, they provided instruction to those destined for the US Army Transport Service. From October 1941, the US Navy also created and trained a large body of men to serve in the US Navy Armed Guard, which provided mainly gunners, signalmen and radio operators to help operate weaponry and assist in merchant ship defence.

Above we have already noted the impressive achievements of the US shipbuilding programme during World War II – by the end of the conflict, the Merchant Marine had grown to a strength of 4,221 vessels. Equally inspiring were the levels of manpower recruited and trained for the Merchant Marine: 255,000 by August 1945. In terms of its logistical capability, the Merchant Marine was now the world's premier maritime power.

Costly Victory

Both the Merchant Navy and Merchant Marine were global in their reach and influence. Although the Battle of the Atlantic and the Arctic convoys have occupied much historical attention when it comes to the Merchant Navy, British shipping plied dangerous sea routes around the world, including around Africa, across the Indian Ocean and through the Pacific. The US Merchant Marine also ranged widely, with a particularly huge commitment in the Pacific, where fleets of logistical vessels supported the US-led campaign to reclaim the vast swathes of Japanese-occupied territory.

Wherever the merchant ships served, they faced countless daily threats – mines, air attack (including kamikazes in the Pacific), enemy submarines, surface raiders, to name purely a few tactical threats. Added to this were all the dangers of the sea itself, from mountainous Atlantic storms through to simple, and common, falls overboard. (In convoy, if a man fell overboard and the convoy did not have destroyer escorts present, the convoy ships were forbidden to turn around the pick the man up.) The peak year for Allied merchant ship destruction was 1942, in which 1,662 ships were lost in all theatres, the peak largely the result of German U-boats enjoying a second 'Happy Time' targeting inexperienced US merchant crews off the coast of the United States.

But despite these dangers, by the end of 1943 until the final months of the war, life became progressively safer for the merchant ship crews. The Allies steadily gained air supremacy in all theatres, which reduced the levels of maritime air attacks. More significantly, the war against the U-boats was won through a combination of new weapons and detection technologies, improved escort tactics, far greater numbers of escort vessels, transatlantic air cover and codebreaking triumphs, plus the Germans' loss of their French U-boat stations to the Allied land advance in 1944–45. Thus in 1945, just 103 Allied merchant vessels were lost in all theatres.

The cost of the war for the merchant maritime service was sobering, with percentage losses in excess of most regular combat forces. Accurate casualty figures are quite difficult to come by, but some of the best figures indicate that in the Merchant Navy 36,749 men and women died as a result of enemy action. If we then add the 5,720 taken prisoner and the 4,707 wounded, we arrive at the conclusion that about a quarter of all Merchant Navy personnel who served during the war became casualties. This casualty rate is only exceeded by the personnel of RAF Bomber Command. For the Merchant Marine, the figures aren't as severe, but equally speak of heavy human suffering – c. 6,000–9,000 dead, plus 12,000 wounded and 600 prisoners.

Life in the merchant navies had little glamour, offering punishing physical labour and the very high chance of a grim death in distant oceans. Yet the service provided by the crews actually underpinned the very viability of the Allied war effort, a fact that must always be recognised in our debt of gratitude to the wartime generation.

This book, through its collection of wartime maritime manuals and instructions, tries to provide an insight into the merchant mariner's world and concerns, from basic principles of seamanship through to how to survive a ship sinking. Collecting this information has presented its challenges. While the US Navy, Coast Guard and Merchant Marine were generally better at creating documents and manuals relating to merchant ship service, the British were rather more ad hoc in their approach. Thus the British documents here are a mix of official and semi-official publications, Admiralty instructions, lectures and notes. We must always remind ourselves that much of the knowledge acquired by sailors in merchant service was informal and acquired on-the-job, and this can be reflected in the sources. What was certain was that the sailors on wartorn seas had to learn a new set of tactical, defensive and survival skills very quickly, if they were to raise their chances of seeing the end of the war.

CHAPTER I

MERCHANT SHIP CREWS AND
BASIC SEAMANSHIP

In 1940, the publisher Sampson Low, Marston & Co. Ltd produced a hardback small-format but lengthy (570 pages) book entitled *His Majesty's Merchant Navy*. This extensive work, compiled and edited by Lieutenant-Commander E. C. Talbot Booth, was to a large extent to encourage recruitment as much as explain the Merchant Navy to both public and serving sailors. Over the course of its 74 chapters it detailed not only the history of the Merchant Navy, but also the roles, ranks and responsibilities of crews, rates of pay, the types of vessels, and reflections (without giving away any combat-sensitive secrets) on the use of the convoy system. As such the book provides an extremely useful snapshot of the Merchant Navy service in the early years of the war.

The book also provided two chapters on merchant sailor training. Merchant sailors from the pre-war years brought with them a vast collected experience, and indeed many ex-seaman were recruited as instructors to impart the basic skills that would be vital to onboard efficiency. Many new officers, by contrast, were trained at one of three naval colleges – HMS *Conway* off Birkenhead in the Mersey; HMS *Worcester* on the Thames in London; and Pangborne on the Berkshire Downs. For the lower ranks, most seaman learnt their trade on the job, rising up to able-bodied seaman status following years of service as a deck hand. Teenage wartime recruits were also sent to various training ships dotted around the country, there to be instructed in the fundamental skills of seamanship, particularly navigation, boat handling, rope tying, naval law and etiquette and safety.

Our first extract is from *His Majesty's Merchant Navy*. It provides a concise understanding of ranks and roles aboard a typical merchant ship, and hence an insight into the diverse spectrum of skills possessed by a sizeable crew. Naturally the crew levels would vary substantially according to the type of vessel, with small fishing boats or tugs, for example, having just three or four men aboard. Whatever the size of the boat, however, all duties – from navigating the ship to completing official paperwork – had to be performed by someone competent.

His Majesty's Merchant Navy (1940)

CHAPTER VIII
A Ship's Officers and Their Duties

IT is difficult to lay down hard and fast rules about the number of officers carried by a ship and their various duties because they must both necessarily vary very considerably according to the size and class of vessel. Conditions differ again according to the trade on which she is engaged.

Under the Board of Trade regulations a minimum number is laid down for officers and crew, and in the past some shipowners have only too frequently rigidly adhered to this minimum, so that while they are keeping the letter of the law, they are working their personnel over-hard, and officers, particularly, who until recent times had nobody to fight their case, were over-worked and had a most uncomfortable time. The large, well established firms, on the other hand, usually have a better reputation and it is only fair to say that conditions have improved all round.

There are still too many cases of ships carrying uncertificated officers or officers of other than British nationality, both of which classes naturally are less expensive to provide. Officers in ships carrying native crews almost invariably have to have a very good working knowledge of their language and most are fluent in it. British ships trading round the China coasts almost all have white officers and Chinese crews. As a guide one cannot do better than take the number of officers in a passenger liner of about 20,000 tons.

It must always be borne in mind that Merchant Navy officers command by their example and character. They have no Naval Discipline Act to back them up in enforcing orders, and the crew, although generally splendid fellows, have not the rigid training or discipline of the Royal Navy behind them. That the standard of discipline is so high is a testimony to the conduct of the officers.

Commodore or Commodore Captain

The senior Master in a British shipping company is usually accorded the courtesy title of Commodore. Some lines have always had one and others have had periods when the title has fallen into abeyance. Such officers fly a Commodore's Flag which is usually the company's House Flag in the shape of a burgee. His command is nearly always the largest and newest in the fleet and is designated the "Flagship".

Captain, Commander or Master

The supreme authority. Responsible for the safe navigation of the ship and for the conduct and efficiency of his junior officers and of the whole of the personnel under his command. He is responsible for the comfort and well-being of his passengers, if carried.

Master Mariner

is still his correct title and this dates from the old days when there was little difference in build between ships of war and merchant ships. Soldiers were carried to do the fighting and the sailors looked after the navigation of the ships. The Captain was the head of the troops and the Master was the head of the seamen. A man who holds a Master's Certificate but who has never held a command should not use nor be addressed by the title of Captain. In most large liners all the Navigating Officers hold Masters' Certificates regardless of their actual position on board. The Commander is known as "The Skipper" or "The Old Man" to his crew.

Staff Captain

Many of the large liners carry a Staff Captain whose duties may be likened to those of a Commander in a ship-of-war. The senior Executive Officer and the right-hand man of the Commander, he is frequently entirely responsible for the navigation, but the Master is always the ultimate authority. It is the proud tradition of the Merchant Navy that the Master is the last to leave his ship when she is in danger. In bad weather or times of anxiety he keeps to the bridge, sometimes for days at a stretch, with occasional snatches of sleep in the chart-room.

Chief Officer

If a Staff Captain is not carried, the Chief Officer acts in the same capacity. He is responsible for the smooth working of the entire ship, is in charge of the entire upper deck personnel and more often than not in charge of or responsible for the cargo. He does not stand watches.

First Officer

Comes next below the Chief Officer if carried, or, in smaller ships, next to the Master. Under him are the Second, Third and Fourth Officers who are the actual watch-keeping officers.

Frequently there are Senior Seconds, Junior Seconds and so on. In smaller ships there is no First Officer and the Second comes next to the Chief Officer.

In Board of Trade parlance all these officers are Mates and were formerly spoken of and to, as "Mister".

Watches are usually kept by a senior and junior officer together, the senior being O.O.W., and during his term of duty he is responsible for the navigation and safety of the ship although the Master bears the final responsibility. The O.O.W. receives periodical reports from the ship's police, the carpenters and stewards regarding their different departments. All navigational, bridge and engine room instruments, telegraphs, etc., are tested during the watch and all water-tight doors, fire alarms and safety valves are inspected at regular intervals.

Lamp-trimmers at night report all navigational lights burning every half-hour and any change of course or unexpected events have to be reported to the Master. Daily the Master "goes rounds", that is, he makes an inspection of the ship attended by the Purser, the Engineer Officer and sometimes by the Surgeon. All the above gives but a very brief outline of duties.

Cadet, Midshipman or Apprentice

All ships do not carry these junior officers who are either sent direct to sea under the "Apprentice" system or else come from one of the Colleges or Training Ships. In the former case the apprentice is indentured to the company for a term of years and a premium is paid to the shipowner to teach him his job. This is returned in wages. The system is gradually dying out in favour of the properly trained junior coming from the Colleges who enters direct as Junior Officer in most cases.

In many instances in the past the youngster had to pick up what he could on the voyage. He was frequently employed entirely on seaman's duties or in cleaning brass-work, and the only opportunities that he had for acquiring knowledge depended upon the goodwill of the Master and officers, who, however well intentioned, had little time to spare to train juniors. The system of entry is gradually becoming standardised and they receive a thorough training, especially in some companies such as the Federal, for example, whose ships have accommodation for a good many cadets. Being cargo ships only, but of the largest and finest type, there is plenty of time to regularise a proper system of training and instruction, much as in a training cruiser of the Royal Navy.

Cadets take their turn with the watch-keepers and in addition they have to make a thorough study of the lay-out of their ship and draw up weird and wonderful charts showing the stowage of cargo and the position of valves, water-tight doors and so on.

So much for upper-deck officers.

Engineer Officers
In complete command in the engine-room is the Chief Engineer, or "Chief" as he is usually spoken of. He is responsible only to the Master. There is in large ships usually an Assistant Chief Engineer, but in the Merchant Navy there is never a First Engineer. Next come Second, Third and Fourth Engineers, who all take shares in engine-room watches. It must be remembered that all the auxiliary and refrigerating machinery comes under this department.

Lighting, ventilating and water supplies are, needless to say, of prime importance, and complaints by passengers that their bath or shaving water is not up to the right temperature, have all to be borne by the engineers.

Surgeons
These officers vary according to the size of ship and the number of passengers carried. Ships carrying more than twelve passengers must carry a certificated Surgeon or "M.O." [medical orderly] The senior surgeon usually remains with the company for many years and under him may be a junior who is travelling to gain experience before settling down in shore practice.

There may also be at least one Nursing Sister and she and all the medical comforts come under the charge of the M.O.

There have been many instances of Ship Surgeons giving professional advice by wireless to some ship not carrying one and many other cases in which they have gone across to another vessel, often through heavy seas, in order to perform an operation or to give personal attention. The Surgeons may not receive any fees from passengers.

Purser
This hard-worked officer has charge of all the clerical and victualling work in a ship, both of passengers and crew. Under him may be an Assistant Purser or a Deputy Assistant or a Deputy Purser and several Assistant Pursers or "A.P.s.'

It has often been said that Pursers are born, not made, and judging by some com. panies this must be true. To reach perfection one has to be a superman, diplomat and managing director rolled into one. In some companies it is said that "Pursers may come and Pursers may go, but the company goes on forever".

It is a well-known fact that travelling in any shape or form, brings out the worst in a person, and judging by the conduct of some pasengers in ships, this is certainly true. They are usually well fed, well housed, kept amused and pampered and have nothing to do but "grouse".

Board of Trade, Customs and Health Authorities all have to be satisfied by the filling in of innumerable forms. Immigration officials have to be provided with full details and passports of intending settlers and crews have to be paid.

Statistics have to be kept of all goods consumed, and sometimes a certain Director may expect the most extraordinary additional statistics kept for his own personal benefit.

All passengers ventilate their complaints or requests at the Purser's Office, which is usually open at certain hours only. Because of this no doubt the universal opinion has grown up that the Purser and his staff have little to do. The facts are, that as in banks, the real hard work is done when closed to the public.

All shore excursions are arranged by the Purser's staff. Orchestras, sports committees and stewards are all in the same department. The mail is handled by the same quarter and valuables may be left in charge. Money is exchanged into foreign currency. In short, over and above the general routine of the ship herself, the entire welfare and comfort of the passengers is the care of the Purser.

Rates of Pay of Ships' Officers
Pay varies according to the company and according to years of service, and it is impossible to give anything but a general idea for the sake of interest.

It can be said that when a cadet has finished his service with a company and is promoted to Junior Officer he will receive a salary of from between £130 to £150 a year. Junior or Third Officers in a passenger ship receive from £144–£252 provided that they hold Master's Certificates.

Second Officers	£144–£300
First Officers	£180–£460
Chief Officers	£250–£600
Captain	£500–£1,000
Commodore	£1,500

Promotion in liner companies is slow and goes very largely by seniority.

In cargo ships the rates of pay are lower than those above, and here is an idea: Second Officer, £170–£227; First Officer, £227–£300; Masters, £300–£800.

Promotion of Officers and Board of Trade Certificates

Year by year the standard required by the various Board of Trade examinations becomes higher. New and more stringent regulations again came into force at the beginning of 1930.

There are four certificates in all.

Before a cadet may present himself for his first examination, that is for the Second Mate's Certificate, he must have reached his twentieth birthday, and have served not less than four years at sea, of which at least four-fifths must be served away from a home port. Two years at one of the recognised Training Ships or Colleges is allowed to count as one complete year of sea service. This is always providing that the cadet has received the Leaving Certificate.

On obtaining the Second Mate's Certificate an officer is entitled to take charge of a watch. After eighteen months' sea service in charge of a watch he may present himself for his First Mate's "ticket". After a further eighteen to thirty months, according to the rank held on board in the interval, a man may sit for his Master's Certificate. Possession of an Extra Master's Certificate does not carry with it any definite advancement, but it enables the holder to apply for special positions for which it may be demanded. It is held by a majority of Masters.

The Board of Trade have full powers to deprive an officer of his certificate or to suspend it for a period if, in their judgment, he is considered to have failed in his duties as a seaman or to have failed to take all reasonable courses of action. After every loss of a British ship or serious casualty, a Board of Trade inquiry is held to inquire into the cause and to apportion blame as necessary.

Wireless Officers and The Marconi Company

Wireless Officers or "Sparks" are not, strictly speaking, members of the British Merchant Navy. They are employees of the Marconi International Marine Radio Co. They receive their training in shore establishments and are "lent" by the company to the shipping lines, and so may remain with one ship or company for a considerable time, or, if they choose, may serve in many ships in the course of a few years.

At the time of the introduction of the Standard pattern uniform in 1918 for the Merchant Navy, a pattern was also authorised for wireless operators. This consists of wavy stripes as shown on another page. The cap badge is that of the Marconi Company. Although not belonging to the sea service, Wireless Officers have built up, in a comparatively short time, a high tradition of devotion to duty. It was only in the early years of this century that wireless or radio was first adopted in ships, and even before the last war it was almost in its infancy.

If there is not always an operator actually in the wireless cabin or room, an automatic alarm is connected to the officer's cabin so that at all times of day or night there is a constant watch.

One of the earliest examples of gallantry was performed by the operator of *Titanic*, who continued to send out distress calls until the end; and instances since, both in war and in peace, have become too numerous to recount.

The Wireless Officer is gladly accepted as a worthy colleague by all ranks of the Service.

[. . .]

Chapter X
The Crew of a Merchant Ship

THE majority of the crew of a large merchant ship carrying passengers primarily, consists of those in the Stewards' department. The upper-deck personnel is comparatively small. Ranks are the same as those in the Royal Navy as a general rule, although there are no Warrant Officers, unless such people as Chief Stewards may be said to take their place. Nor, naturally, are there so many non-substantive ratings, although there are cooks, printers, deck stewards, mess-room waiters and so on.

The Chief Petty Officer is the Boatswain who comes between the officers and the men. For this reason he has acquired the nickname of "Chief Buffer" or "Buffer. It is a very old title, dating back to Viking days, and comes from "Boats' Swain", meaning that he has to "husband" or look after the crew. He and his subordinates take charge of the seamen and superintend all working parties.

The Master-at-Arms is head of the ship's police, and patrols the passenger decks as well. He takes control at the gangways to keep an eye on undesirable elements and sometimes has to eject too-persistent natives who pester passengers with their wares.

The Baggage Master has, as his name implies, entire charge of stowage and removal of passengers' personal packages. His life is not always a happy one, as passengers frequently endeavour to get permission to extract articles packed in the "Not wanted on voyage" rooms. He has to stow it in such a manner that passengers disembarking at intermediate ports suffer no inconvenience, and the stay in such ports does not allow of much delay.

The highest rank of seaman is Able-Bodied Seaman (A.B.), although some may be given the rating of Leading Seaman. This group provides the Quartermaster, who takes charge of the wheel, and strangely enough Chinamen seem to make very good quartermasters, perhaps because they seem to be able to concentrate better than the average European.

Next come the Ordinary Seamen (O.S.), and then the Boy Ratings, who act as messengers, signallers and so on.

More and more attention is being devoted to the training of efficient Signalmen, and it is very necessary.

This about completes the list of upper-deck personnel.

King of the catering department is the Chief Steward. Sometimes he ranks as an officer, and he is very frequently taken for one by passengers, as he is always in evidence on embarkation days, usually flitting around the gangways.

In ships which do not carry a Purser, all the clerical work is performed by the Chief Steward.

As of the Purser, it is frequently said with truth that a good Chief Steward is born. he can never be made unless he has the necessary gifts. In some Lines it is said that the Directors would rather lose a Captain than a good Chief Steward.

There are numerous Deputy or Assistant Stewards, according to the size of the ship.

Under the Chief Steward come all the waiters for dining saloons, cabins and deck. The entire provisioning and catering is in his hands.

In the engine-room there are the Firemen, and Stokers. In the days of oil-fired boilers and motor ships, the number is getting less than before, and the place of the less-skilled man is being taken by the scientifically trained.

The task of stoking a ship is a very difficult one, and the idea that any idiot can perform it is very wrong. Not only is a great amount of strength and physical endurance necessary, but in addition, very great skill is required to furnish an even and regular supply of fuel to the furnaces.

Many of the ships on the Eastern runs have all, or a large proportion, of the engine-room staff furnished by native seamen. Some of the big Lines also employ native seamen in the Stewards' departments.

As a matter of interest the number of crew carried by a few representative types of British ships is appended:

Queen Mary (express passenger and mail N. Atlantic liner)	1,100
Viceroy of India (P. & 0. 20,000 tons Eastern liner)	
(Made up of about 110 deck department, 75 engine-room,	
and the rest stewards' and pursers' department.)	600
Worcestershire (11,000 tons, "First-class only")	200
Beaver Class (10,000 tons cargo liner)	80
8,000 ton tanker	40
5,000 ton tramp ship	35

Rates of Pay of the Crew of a British Merchant Ship

The standard rates of pay obtaining at the outbreak of the war in September, 1939, are set out below.

Over and above these a war risk bonus of £5 monthly is paid, with half rate for boy ratings. The rates of pay vary somewhat according to whether the man is employed on the home, coastal or foreign trade and according to the tonnage or number of passengers carried.

Pay in tankers is slightly in excess of that shown.

Ordinary Seaman	£5 16s. 3d. *monthly* to £7 7s. 6d.
Able Seaman	£10 12s. 6d. monthly or £13 8s. 6d. if they find their own food.
Boatswain	£12 10s. 0d. to £14 15s. 0d.
Fireman	£11 2s. 6d.
Assistant Steward	£9 17s. 6d.

As we have seen, World War II brought the unprecedented expansion of Allied merchant navies, as they attempted both to meet the inexhaustible logistical demands of the war, plus fill the gaps left by the terrible losses inflicted by U-boats and other Axis predators. All new sailors had to learn the fundamental skills of seamanship before they could be assigned to an active crew. Veteran memories of this time indicate that training regimes could be as harsh as anything imposed upon the military services. One mariner, who joined at age 16, remembers a five-week induction course aboard a grim training ship moored permanently in London. The course consisted of:

Week 1 – Learning to 'box to compass' (to know and recite the 32 points and quarter points of the magnetic compass from North, both clockwise and anticlockwise)
Week 2 – Learning the techniques of knots and splicing
Week 3 – Managing cargo and stowing lifeboat equipment
Week 4 – Boat handling (basic sailing techniques)
Week 5 – Lifeboat drill

Of course, a five-week programme of instruction did not make for an experienced mariner, and many of the essential skills would have to be learned through subsequent service aboard a ship.

The training for the US Merchant Marine service appears more substantial. From 1938, when the Maritime Service was formed, the US Coast Guard was the primary training agency, the programmes delivered via seven main training centres and two officer candidate centres. For those who already had experience at sea, the training programmes lasted about three months, while for new members with no experience, six months of training were given.

The first manual used here is exactly the sort of text on which the US recruits would rely. Published in 1943, the *United States Maritime Service Training Manual, Deck Branch Training* manual was intended largely for those who had no prior knowledge of seamanship. Here we see the basic techniques of the mariner explained. As we shall see, there was a lot to learn.

United States Maritime Service Training Manual:
Deck Branch Training **(1943)**

STEERING

For some mysterious reason, the word "helm" still survives even though it has been prohibited by an act of Congress along with the words "port" and "starboard" in connection with steering. All orders used should be direct; "right rudder" meaning to turn the wheel right so that the head of the ship goes to the right and "left rudder" meaning to turn the wheel left so that the head of the ship goes to the left.

Much confusion has arisen due to some men being instructed at wheel commands conforming to Navy methods. Thus "left 100" under Navy commands would mean to turn the wheel until the rudder angle indicator showed left 10°. However on merchant ships the order "left 10°" would ordinarily mean steer a course 10° to the left of the one you are now steering. Orders to the wheel should be interpreted according to merchant marine practice unless otherwise notified. For example under Navy commands, 10° right is an abbreviation of 10° right rudder.

The maximum angle of turning efficiency is about 35°. Never attempt to force a wheel over any further than 35°.

When the ship is swinging you may receive the order "ease the wheel." This means to bring your wheel back slowly to amidships, making sure you do not check the swing of the ship. If, however, you receive the order, "Steady" or "Steady as she goes," immediately check the swing of the ship and steady her on the course she was heading when you received the order.

Ordinarily the man conning the ship relies a great deal on the good judgment of the man at the wheel. As a result, to a beginner, his commands may seem rather indefinite. Such commands might be, "left a little," "left some more," "don't let her come too fast" and "keep her in the middle." Every opportunity for observing experienced helmsmen in pilot waters should be taken by the beginner so that he may recognize what is meant by these terms. As long as you stay out of the way and are not using up ship's time no objection will be made to your remaining on the bridge for this purpose. It is always best, however, to first obtain permission from the mate on watch.

Many pilots and captains give their orders by waving their hands and arms in the direction they wish the wheel turned. For this reason it is important to keep your eyes on the person conning. A wave to the left indicates left wheel, one to the right, right wheel and an up-and-down motion indicates "steady."

With the wheel left, another wave to the left would mean "more left wheel," whereas one to the right would mean "ease the wheel."

Regardless of whether orders are given in this manner or by voice, the helmsman should repeat each order in a clear, distinct voice. Do not change the wording of any command but repeat exactly as given.

When relieving the wheel always attempt to relieve five minutes ahead of time. This will be appreciated by your shipmates. Find out if it is customary to bring the mate on watch any coffee when coming to the wheel, and if this is the practice find out from him how he likes his coffee. The man at the wheel gives the course (both magnetic and gyro, if a gyro is aboard) to his relief, steadies the ship on the course and then hands the watch over. He in turn approaches the mate on watch, repeats the course (example: 125° per gyro, 129° per magnetic) and after the mate repeats, he goes below. A good man coming off the wheel will always pick up any cups or other items which should go below. He will also give his relief some idea of how the ship is steering, (example: half a right turn and no left wheel).

A seaman at the wheel of a modern Liberty ship.

The man coming to the wheel should spend the first five minutes of his watch getting the feel of the ship and determining how much wheel is required to keep the ship on its course. Remember changes in course, wind, or sea will affect the steering so you must be attentive and concentrate on your job which is steering. If your ship has a gyro compass it will be part of your job to check it with the magnetic whenever course is changed, and at least every half hour when the course is not changed. Should you obtain a different comparison, notify the mate instantly as the gyro may have failed. If steering by magnetic and you find the compass acting strangely report it to the mate on watch.

Do not confuse the expression "what's your course" and "how do you head" or "what's your head?" The first is a question to find out what course you are supposed to be heading. By the second question the mate desires information as to the ship's head at that precise moment. In this case do not be vague with your answer. For example, your course is 130°, the mate asks, "How do you head?" You note the compass as reading 127°. Report in a clear voice, "127° sir, 3° to the left," (meaning, of course, you are 3° off the course you should be steering).

No hard fast rules for steering can be laid down, however these points are set down in the hope they will be of some help:

1. Under ordinary conditions (small wind and sea) a ship will require little right wheel and no left wheel. This is due to the fact that ships are fitted with right-hand propellers which throw the ship's head to the left.
2. With moderate wind and sea ahead or astern, the ship will take a little right and a little left wheel.
3. With moderate wind and sea on the starboard bow, the ship will take a little left and no right wheel as she has a tendency to come up into the wind.
4. **Remember** the lubber's line is the line you must move. Do not attempt to move the compass around to the lubber's line. If the lubber's line is to right of course, turn wheel left; if lubber's line is to left of course, turn wheel right.

In heavy weather the yawing of the ship may confuse a new helmsman into putting his wheel over unnecessarily. Watch the compass and if the ship swings away from the course and then returns to it or past it, do not give her any wheel. If, however, the ship does not return to the course, she is falling off and you must give her some wheel.

Ordinarily steering is done by the compass, the course being given in degrees. As you become more proficient you will find you can steer a better course by watching the ship's head. At sea a stationary cloud or even the horizon may be watched for the swing. In pilot waters steering by ship's head becomes very important. When given a course to steer or given the order "Steady," pick out a prominent object ahead and steer for it. Many harbors and rivers are fitted with ranges for this purpose, but houses, trees, hills, smokestacks, tanks, or any other conspicuous object may be used.

HELM ORDERS

When you relieve the wheel enter the wheelhouse from lee door. Go quietly and directly to the helmsman standing close and just back of him stating "Wheel relief," (indicating you are ready to take the wheel). The helmsman will then steady the ship on his last assigned course and put the wheel amidships. As he turns the wheel over to you he states the course being steered, the numbers of degrees helm she is carrying to keep steady on course and that the wheel is amidship in this manner. "Course, one eight zero (180°), wheel amidship." Or he may add the added information, and should, so you will steer a better course and become accustomed to the ship's actions or steering, "Carrying a half left wheel" or right, as the case may be, to make her steady better. The relieving helmsman then repeats just what he has heard and in the same order.

The relieved helmsman then steps over to the mate on watch giving the course he has been steering and turns it over to his relief to steer. Example: "Wheel relieved, sir, course one eight zero (180°)." The officer will then reply, "Very well," and with the same course you have just given, if you have turned over the wheel correctly and with correct course. When he repeats the same course as you have given he indicates you have been correct and if there is no further comment you immediately and quietly leave the bridge through the lee door.

Note that on the relief of the wheel the course has been given and repeated three times. There is an object to this which can readily be seen. If the course is not repeated as given the man in error must be corrected. In other words, if you repeat correctly you signify you understand, for example:

Relieving man: Stands close behind helmsman stating, "Wheel relief."

Helmsman: After steadying on course and wheel amidship: "Course one zero five (105°). Wheel amidship."

Relief: "One zero five (105°). Wheel amid-ship."

Relieved helmsman, going to officer on watch: "Wheel relieved, sir, course or steering one zero five (105°)."

Mate on watch: "Very well, course one zero five (105°)."

Relieved helmsman then leaves the bridge through lee door if no further orders.

ORDERS ARE AS FOLLOWS

Right wheel – Turn wheel to the right.

Left wheel – Turn wheel to the left.

Right a bit – Turn wheel to right a bit or approximately one turn.

Left a bit – Same as above, only left.

Half right – Turn wheel half the number of turns to right it takes to put the wheel hard right or hard over. If it takes 6 turns to put the wheel "hard right" then "half right" means 3 turns.

Half left – Same as above, only to left.

Amidships or 'midships – Means put the wheel amidship so that the rudder indicator shows the rudder is amidship or in other words rudder is fore and aft or in line with keel.

Ease the wheel – If you had the wheel at hard right, to ease the wheel means to ease it back to the direction of amidships. In other words, take some of the wheel off her. The only way possible to go in "easing the wheel" is toward amidships. It is only possible to ease the wheel right or left to amidship because when you go beyond this point you are putting opposite helm on her as you can see when you pass the amid-ship mark.

"Steady as you go" or "Steady"– Means that as the command is given you note the course and work the wheel to keep the ship on the course noted at the order of "Steady" until you are given some new helm command or course. If in a harbor, steady on some fixed and easily seen object ahead to help keep the vessels head steady but don't fail to note the compass course also. It is easier to steady the vessel on an object ahead; such as a range, stack or some prominent object ashore when in harbors or inland waters than to steer by compass course alone. Of course at sea you must steer by compass course.

Hard right or left – This means putting the wheel over to the direction given as far as it will go.

In closing, the need for expert steering in wartime must be emphasized. Poor steering may result in collision and on dark nights it may mean getting out of the convoy. Running at 9 knots, a ship steering a course 3° different than the rest of the convoy in six minutes will move the ship 300' out of its station. Imagine this course steered for the entire night and you can easily see why some ships lose the convoy.

When you are directly exposed to very bright or tropical sunshine, excessive light may enter your eyes either directly from the sun or by direct reflection from snow, ice, sand, or water. The immediate result is apt to be excessive production of tears, spasm of the lids, and marked irritation. For protection against the direct rays of the sun you should wear a broad-brimmed hat or helmet. For protection against excessive light reflected from water, ice, sand or snow, sunglasses are essential. The lenses of these glasses should not only be suited for their purpose of absorbing unwanted radiation but they should also be free of irregularities and optical defects which may be the cause of eyestrain if the sunglasses are worn for long periods.

In view of the fact that in doing all close eye work the muscles of the eye must be in almost continuous activity, it is evident that excessive fatigue of these muscles is very common. To reduce the "wear and tear" on these muscles and increase their reserves, the following suggestions will be found helpful:

(a) obtain as far as possible an adequate amount of sleep;
(b) do not expect your eyes to have their normal visual reserve when you are physically overtired or have been forced to reduce markedly your hours of sleep;
(c) in doing close eye work arrange for proper illumination (adequate in intensity and directed from behind) and rest your eyes by looking up from the close work and looking away at a distance, if possible, at frequent intervals;
(d) be moderate in the reading of newspaper print or other difficult print at night when you are already tired.

[. . .]

THE COMPASS

The compass is the most important navigation instrument used by mariners. It is the instrument by which the mariner finds his direction.

There are two types of compasses. The magnetic compass and the gyro compass.

The magnetic compass depends upon the natural magnetism of the earth for its directive force. Basically it consists of a magnetic needle or needles free to turn on a pivot. Obeying the laws of magnetism, the needle is attracted toward the poles and remains in that direction. The north pole of the needle being attracted to the north magnetic pole of the earth.

The magnetic compass as now used at sea, consists of a bowl swinging level in gimbals and a group of highly magnetized steel needles attached to a graduated card all mounted on a pivot in the center of the bowl. A vertical line called a lubber's line is marked on the inner surface of the bowl and the compass is so mounted in the ship that a line through the lubber's line and the pivot is parallel with the ship's keel. Thus, the lubber's line indicates the ship's head, and the reading on the graduated card opposite the lubber's line indicates the compass course of the ship.

The more modern magnetic compasses have the bowl filled with liquid. This tends to reduce the weight on the pivot and also dampens the effect of the vibration, pitching, and rolling of the ship.

Some dry compasses are still in use and they do have certain advantages, the main one probably being the ease with which the card of the compass is changed. Because the full weight of the card and needles rests on the pivot it is of very light construction, the card usually being of light paper.

The magnetic compass is subject to two errors, variation, and deviation. Variation is the error due primarily to the difference between the magnetic and geographic poles. Deviation is an error due to the magnetic qualities of the steel within a ship.

The gyro compass is a mechanical compass that derives its directive force from the fact that a gyro tends to line its axis parallel to that of the earth. Its direction except for slight mechanical errors is, therefore, true. Since a gyro compass is mechanical and therefore subject to mechanical failure it is important that it is checked frequently with the magnetic compasses kept aboard ship. The biggest advantage of the gyro compass is the fact that its directive force is so powerful that it can be used to operate any number of repeater compasses situated throughout the ship. These repeaters will read exactly as the master compass.

DIVISION OF THE COMPASS CARD

There are various ways of dividing the compass card and the well-informed seaman should understand each.

The modern and probably the most common method of dividing the card is into 360°, from 0° at the north point around clockwise or to the right and all the way around to 360° which is again at 0°.

An older method and one still used occasionally is by points. In this method the compass is divided into 32 points of 11 1/4° each and these are further divided into quarter points of 2° 48' 45" each.

Another system not used much anymore but still one a seaman should understand is the 90° or quadrant card. In this system the course never exceeds 90° and directions so given require letters to indicate the quadrant, thus; Northeast, by points – 45° by the 360° compass card– N 45° E by the quadrant card or Northwest, by points – 315° by the 360° card – N 45° W by the quadrant card, etc.

Although most ships are now equipped with the 360° card it is important that a seaman knows and fully understands the other various cards and be able to translate from one to the other very quickly. It is not uncommon to find pilots in certain ports and even some officers that find it convenient to use one of the older systems when giving courses and it is up to the man at the wheel to prove his knowledge of the compass.

North	East	South	West
N by E	E by S	S by W	W by N
NNE	ESE	SSW	WNW
NE by N	SE by E	SW by S	NW by W
NE	SE	SW	NW
NE by E	SE by S	SW by W	NW by N
ENE	SSE	WSW	NNW
E by N	S by E	W by S	N by W

LOOKOUT DUTY

Too much emphasis can never be placed upon the importance of the lookout on shipboard. This is particularly true in time of war. Many accidents at sea could have been avoided if the lookout had been alert and attentive.

If you are on lookout you must report anything that comes into sight. This includes other ships, lights, land, shoals, discolored water, buoys, floating objects, periscopes, and wreckage. In short, report anything that might be of interest to the bridge, even garbage or refuse.

Lookouts are stationed on the forecastle head in the crow's nest and in time of war frequently on the stern and other parts of the vessel.

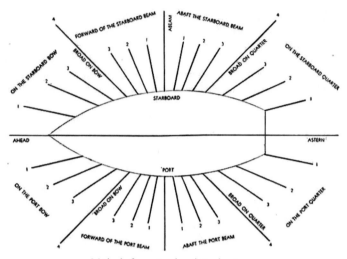

Method of reporting by relative bearings.

The report when on the forecastle head is usually made by the striking of the ship's bell (on some vessels it is made by speaking tube or telephone). One bell signifies an object is sighted to the starboard. Two bells implies that an object is sighted to the port. Three bells indicates an object dead ahead of your ship. This report will be acknowledged by the officer on the bridge. If no acknowledgement is made, repeat the signal until understood and acknowledged.

Frequently additional description of objects sighted may be required. This may include the position of the object with relation to the ship (relative bearing). The accompanying illustration gives you a clear picture of the manner in which this is accomplished. Report in points or degrees. A report in degrees is preferable because of its greater accuracy.

When you sight something, supplement the proper signal on the ship's bell by singing out in a loud, clear voice. For example-You have just struck one bell. Immediately following this you sing out, "Wreckage and oil slick, three points on the starboard bow, sir."

The common failing among inexperienced lookouts is their method of scanning the horizon or sky. Generally an inexperienced man concentrates his attention in one particular direction, usually dead ahead, with now and then a quick glance around the ship. Such a method will almost always result in the lookout not seeing a small object or distant plane. Lookouts should practice slow scanning in sectors with a quick return to the starting place (see illustration). Each new sector scanned should overlap the last sector examined.

Lookouts should be extremely careful in scanning the water between the ship and the horizon. A submarine's periscope may be picked up by an alert lookout at a distance of two miles, and a torpedo wake may be seen at a distance of one mile. During periods of low visibility it may be generally assumed that a submarine will not attack at a greater range than 1,000 yards or 1/2 mile. It can therefore be easily seen the great necessity for carefully scanning those waters about the ship as well as the horizon.

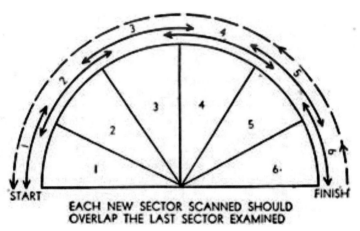

EACH NEW SECTOR SCANNED SHOULD
OVERLAP THE LAST SECTOR EXAMINED

Approved method of scanning for lookout.

Due to the strain on a man's eyes, lookouts should be relieved as often as possible. In order to relax the eyes, lookouts should close their eyes for 10 or 15 seconds about every 20 or 30 minutes. These short periods of rest will prove of great benefit.

When being relieved always point out all objects that have been reported to the bridge. Otherwise, after you have left your relief will pick up the object and report it again. This results in a temporary confusion on the bridge, the mate on watch thinking that a new object is being reported. At night do not be in a hurry to leave post. Give your relief a chance to adjust his eyes to the darkness. The man going on duty should make it a point that the watch is being properly handed over to him. If the ship is showing lights, check to make sure they are operating. If you go on lookout and do not find the man you are to relieve on his station, do not assume he got tired and turned in. Report the fact to the bridge, as the man may have fallen overboard. Make a search of the forecastle head, but do not leave your post. For example, you might see an object on the starboard side, halfway between your fore-and-aft line and your beam. You would report such an object by ringing one bell, and in a loud clear voice reporting, "Ship sighted four points on the starboard bow."

These reports are made by relative bearings from the ship. A relative bearing is a bearing of an object in relation to the ship.

There are thirty-two points in the compass and bearings are reported in terms of the compass. For example, dead ahead, one point on the star-board bow, two points on the starboard bow, three points on the starboard bow, etc.

While on lookout be particularly alert and attentive. Pay no attention to anything but your specific job. Never under any circumstances leave your post until you are properly relieved. Report anything you see, even if you are a bit doubtful about it. If something you think you see turns out to be non-existent, you will not be subject to embarrassment or ridicule. It will merely indicate to the officer of the watch that you are an efficient lookout doing your job properly.

As in all other cases involving seamanship, it is wrong to assume that somebody else will do your job for you. Do not assume that the bridge has sighted something, and that therefore there is no point in your reporting it.

In these days of war it is necessary to be on the lookout for anything in the sky, on or under the water, and on the horizon. A good lookout will cover all points of the compass, unless he is directed to perform his lookout duties over a specified arc of horizon.

When you are on lookout duty, remain on your feet and avoid conversation, except that which applies directly to your job. Be absolutely certain that you thoroughly understand your assignment. If you are in doubt, do not hesitate to consult the officer of the watch.

You must repeat the bells from the bridge immediately following their ringing at every half-hour interval. When navigating in water where lights are required to be carried by your ship, you must check to see that they are properly functioning. If they are in order, hail the bridge by saying, "All lights are burning bright, sir." If they are not in order report the deficiency. However, lights are seldom used at sea during these days of war.

A dim light can be seen quicker at night by first looking at the sky above the horizon and by then dropping the eyes to the horizon.

When standing lookout at night be careful that no light shines in your eyes. The lighting of a match or a flashlight before or during your lookout duty causes temporary blindness. This decreases your efficiency. (Read section entitled, How to Use Your Eyes At Night.)

When you are on lookout duty think constantly of your responsibility. You are the ears, as well as the eyes of your ship. In fog or thick weather listen attentively. Report any indication of a vessel or an object afloat. Be especially alert in fog.

There are certain conditions of visibility, weather and sea when experience indicates that attack is less likely than at other times. This does not mean that your vigilance as a lookout should be relaxed in the slightest at such times. While it is true that there is less chance of attack in a rain squall or in fog, it is also true that you have excellent chances of catching the enemy on the surface at close range under these conditions. Many submarines have been destroyed by merchant ships under such conditions.

In the first World War it was found that a plain piece of cardboard tube about 2 feet long and 1 1/2 inches in diameter dipped inside and out in flat black paint and allowed to dry made an excellent "telescope" for lookout work, especially in daytime. While it had no magnifying power it served to shade the eyes, concentrate the field of vision and greatly reduce eyestrain. The present shortage of binoculars and the good results obtained with this simple device in the last war suggests that it be tried again.

Your job as lookout is of the utmost importance in the safety of your ship, its cargo, and its crew.

Remember, when you go on lookout always wear your life preserver. If for any reason, you do not wear your lifesaving suit, keep it with you constantly. Have it immediately available for use. Your life may very well depend on it. Become proficient in donning the suit rapidly under all types of conditions. With constant practice you should be able to put the rubberized suit on properly, in the dark, in about 30 seconds.

By dressing properly in cold or severe weather, you will be a more efficient lookout. Then you can concentrate on the task at hand without having to suffer the distractions of your discomfort.

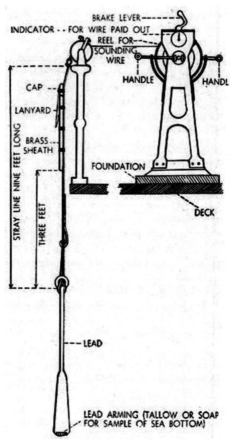

Sounding machine ready for use.

THE SOUNDING MACHINE

For sounding purposes vessels are fitted with a machine consisting of a drum or spool upon which is wound a quantity of fine steel wire.

This wire is made fast to the link which is attached to the lead by a log line. It may be allowed to run out freely or may be reeled in by the proper use of handles attached to the machine.

About a half-turn of the crank in one direction slacks the brake, while the turning of the handle in the opposite direction sets the brake and checks the wire from running out. The depth of water may be determined by means of a depth recorder which has a gage and indicator, or by means of glass tubes, the insides of which are either treated with a chemical preparation or roughened by grinding. The glass tube, protected by a brass case, open at the bottom and attached above the lead. As the lead descends, water is forced into the tube according to pressure of the depth. The water wets the chemical coating or ground interior showing how far the water entered the tube. The discolored or wet portion of the tube measured by a scale, gives the depth.

The machine has a clocklike dial which records the length of wire reeled out. This dial does not indicate accurately the depth of water.

Also after the machine is placed and handles attached, the locking arm is made fast by turning the catch around and the brake is set to prevent the wire running out. The depth recorder or the chemical tube is then adjusted and made fast to a line between the link and the sinker, and the wire made fast to the link.

The attachments are then carefully lowered overboard by hand, and the wire placed in the fair-lead with the link hanging just clear. The wire is then taut and the register on the machine should indicate zero.

When ready to make a cast, a light turn of the handle will release the brake, and the wire is kept taut by pressing upon it by the finger-pin (feeler) which indicates when bottom is reached by a quick slackening of the wire under pressure of the pin. **Do not touch the wire when paying out.**

Watch the indicator and gradually apply the brake before all the wire has passed off the drum or bottom has been reached. Then reverse the motion of the drum and rewind the wire, guiding it on the drum by hand with a piece of waste canvas. Watch until the link is close to the fair-lead and then bring the depth-recorder inboard by hand, carefully keeping it upright until read.

The speed at which the ship is moving determines the length of wire in excess of depth of water required to reach bottom, and great care must be exercised to avoid looping or slacking of the wire and to prevent kinks forming. A kinked wire should be discarded as a slight pull will break it.

HAND LEAD

The hand lead is used for finding the depth of water on entering or leaving a port and in navigating where the depth of water is not over twenty fathoms. It consists of a lead weight of 7 to 14 pounds and a line marked.

In taking soundings with the hand lead the leadsman stands on a platform projecting from the side of the ship, called the chains. The line is held about two fathoms from the end, usually a toggle is provided for this, and the lead is swung to and fro in a fore-and-aft line. When sufficient momentum is obtained the lead is thrown as far forward as possible. An expert leadsman will swing the lead in a complete circle over his head twice before releasing it. As the lead enters the water the slack in the line is taken in until the leadsman feels the lead on the bottom. When the line is stretched out in a straight line up and down, with the lead on the bottom, the sounding is read and called out to the bridge. With practice it is possible to feel the type of bottom and distinguish between a hard, soft or sticky bottom. This information should also be reported to the bridge.

In reporting the soundings to the bridge the following terminology should be used:

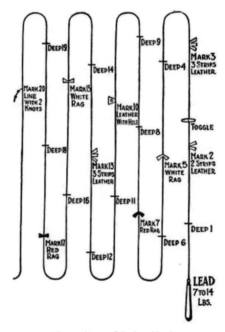

The markings of the hand lead.

When the depth corresponds to any mark on the lead line it is reported as: "By the mark 7," "By the mark 10," etc.

When the depth corresponds to any fathom between the marks on the lead line, it is reported as: "By the deep 6," "By the deep 8."

When the depth is judged to be a fraction greater or less than that indicated by the marks, it is reported as: "And a half 7," "And a quarter 5," "Half less 7," "Quarter less 10."

Lead lines should be marked when wet and frequently checked for accuracy. When taking soundings at night and it is difficult to see the marks, accurate soundings may be taken by reading the line at the rail and subtracting the height of the rail above the water's edge.

MARLINESPIKE SEAMANSHIP

Marlinespike seamanship is a general term covering all phases of ropework. It includes the care, handling, knotting, and splicing of both fibre and wire rope of all sizes. A thorough knowledge of marlinespike seamanship is of the utmost importance to every seaman. It is in constant use on shipboard.

Frequently, the safety of vessel and crew is dependent on knots and splices. For this reason, as a seaman, you must master the methods of quickly tying efficient knots and making splices. Any and every seaman should be able to tie a square knot, half hitches, half hitches with round turn, bowline, clove hitch, bowline on a bight, and timber hitch. You should also be able to make an eye splice and a short splice.

It is desirable to be able to make a long splice as well, although such a splice is not in common usage on modern ships. These days, instead of using a long splice, the line requiring it is renewed. You should be able to make proper mousings and whippings. Also, you should be very familiar with the use of the sailmaker's palm, fid, and marlinespike.

Parts of a rope.

When tying knots, it is customary to speak of different parts of the rope as follows: The end is as the name implies, the very end of the rope. The bight is a loop or half-loop formed by turning the rope back on itself. The standing part is the long unused portion of the rope.

Square knot started and finished.

Square Knot – The square not is the most useful of knots because it is strong, easily tied and untied, and will not slip.

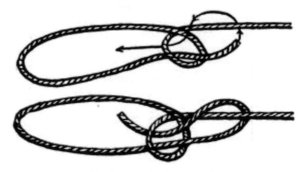

Bowline started and completed.

Bowline – The bowline is the best known and the most useful of the eye knots. It is easily made by forming a bight in the rope and by passing the end up through the bight under the standing part and down through the bight again. A bowline on a bight is a method of making a loop in a rope, both ends of which are fast. Double up the center of a rope and form a double bight. Pass the end of the loop up through this bight. Draw this loop down over the large loop.

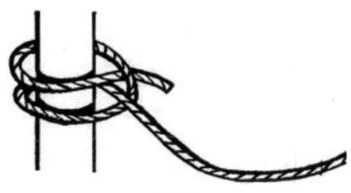

Clove hitch.

Clove Hitch – The clove hitch is used to make a line fast to a spar or post. In this knot the end is passed around twice to form a hitch as illustrated.

Timber hitch.

Timber Hitch – The timber hitch is used where quick fastening is desired as in removing hatch board or dunnage from a hatch. Frequently it is used in combination with a half hitch.

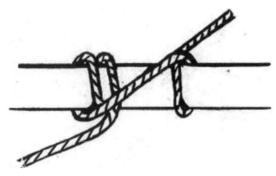

Rolling hitch.

Rolling Hitch – The rolling hitch is used to bend a rope to a spar or to the standing part of another rope. It is principally used as a stopper hitch in stopping off boat falls. This knot is made by passing the end twice around the spar or rope and each time cross the standing part on the top. A hitch around the spar or rope on the opposite side of turns finishes it.

Two half hitches (top) and round turn with two half hitches (bottom).

Two Half Hitches – This is a widely used knot for making a line fast to a spar or ring bolt.

Round Turn with Two Half Hitches – This knot is another method of making a line fast to a spar or ring. It is much more secure than the two half hitches alone. It is used in connection with the Breeches Buoy.

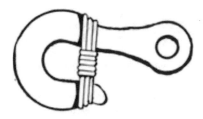

Mousing a hook.

Mousing a Hook – Mousing a hook is a means of preventing a sling or a knot from accidentally coming off a hook.

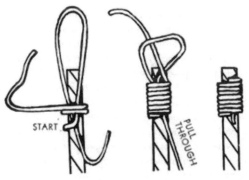

Simple whipping.

Whipping – A whipping is used to prevent the ends of a rope from fraying or becoming unlaid.

Making a line fast to a cleat.

Clips in proper position on wire rope, forming an eye.

Clips shown in the above illustration are used on wire rope to form an eye. The U bolt of all clips should enclose the dead end of the rope.

One variation is the palm and needle whipping which serves the same purpose making for a neater and more permanent job.

SPLICING

It is frequently desirable to fasten two ropes together in a neater manner than can be accomplished by knots. For this purpose various methods of splicing are used. A second advantage of this type of joining is the fact that a well-made splice approaches the strength of the line itself, whereas even the better knots do not.

Small ropes can be spliced by opening the strands with the fingers. For the larger ropes it is useful to have a marlinespike or fid.

Short Splice – In making a short splice, unlay the strands of the two rope ends to be spliced. Then intertwine the strands as shown in the first illustration. Each strand is tucked over and under its companions in the opposing rope ends. After this has been done with all six strands, one round of tucks has been made. Three such rounds of tucks are required for an efficient splice. Remember that in splicing, strands go over and under, over and under.

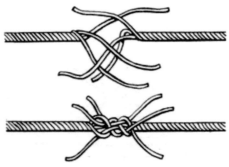

Short splice, started (top) one tuck completed (bottom).

Eye splice with one tuck completed.

Eye Splice – Unlay the rope and from an eye of desired size by bending the crotch of the strand up and the other two strands on either side. Tuck center strand under the strand directly below it; left-hand strand passes over the strand under which the first strand was tucked and then under the next strand. Turn the splice over and twist the last strand with the lay to tighten the yarn and tuck it under the remaining strand. Remember that all strands are tucked from right to left. After you have taken full tucks with the three strands tuck each of them over and under twice more. Although they may appear difficult knots and splices are basically simple. You will find them so if you read this chapter thoroughly and consult the illustrations. That, however, is not enough. To become proficient you must practice constantly. Practice it in your free hours perhaps before you turn in for the night. Bend all the hitches on the guardrail of your bunk, then on the vertical stanchion, then on the overhead pipe. Make knots in the dark too. Be versatile with the use of these basic knots. A few minutes a day, even at sea, will pay by dividends. When you know these knots and splices, how and when to use them, you have accomplished the first phase of your development as a sailor.

CARE AND HANDLING OF ROPE

To open a coil of rope may seem very simple, although you may find yourself in "trouble" with a new line because you did not stop to think before you grabbed an end and blindly started to measure off the amount wanted. To prevent kinks, you must first inspect the coil and locate the inside end. This is within the eye. (By eye is meant the opening in the center of the coil.) Now turn the coil over so that the inside end is down, and reach down to the bottom of the eye and get the inside end and pull it up through the eye. As it comes out it should uncoil in the direction opposite to the movement of the hands of a clock.

The lashings around the coil should be cut from inside the eye and the burlap covering left on the coil. You will find that this keeps coils of rope in shape and consequently a more orderly storeroom.

Remember that rope shrinks in length when wet. If held quite taut when dry, it will be subjected to a great strain in wet weather, sometimes so great that it will break. Slack taut lines when they become wet. Even a heavy dew at night will penetrate an old line and may create a dangerous situation. Slack running rigging at night.

Both heat and moisture will cause rope to deteriorate and lose its strength.

Rope should never be stowed away unless it is perfectly dry, nor should it be covered in a manner that will hold the moisture in.

Rope should be covered whenever possible to protect it from the weather.

Rope should be parcelled with canvas to protect it from chafing at any point where it rubs against a sharp object.

COILING ROPE

To make a straight coil, lay a circular bight of secured end on deck and lay additional bights on top of it using up the entire amount of line: keep out kinks and turns. Capsize entire coil and it will be clear for running.

To flemish down a line, make small circle of free end and continue to lay down circles around it until the total amount of line is down and resembles a coiled clock spring. This is the neatest method.

To flake down, lay out in a straight line, make small circle of free end, then turn back a loop to form a close flat coil and continue to lay flat coils with the ends on top of ends of preceding coil. Always coil a line with the lay.

Right-handed rope should always be coiled in a clockwise direction.

Left-handed rope should always be in a counterclockwise direction.

ROPE TERMS

Becket – A rope eye for the hook of a block. A rope grommet used as a rowlock; any small rope or strap serving as a handle.

Belay – To make fast to a cleat or belaying pin.

Bend – The twisting or turning of a rope so as to fasten it to some object, as a spar or ring.

Bight – Formed by bringing the end of a rope around, near to, or across its own part.

Bitter-end – The last part of a rope; the last link of an anchor chain.

Cable-laid – The same as hawser-laid.

Chafe – To wear the surface of a rope by rubbing against a solid object.

Coil – To lay down rope in circular turns.

End seizing – A round seizing at the end of a rope.

Fid – A tapered wooden pin used to separate the strands when splicing heavy rope.

Hawser-laid– Left-handed rope of nine strands, in the form of three three-stranded, right-handed ropes.

Heart – The inside center strand of a rope.

Heave – To haul or pull on a line; to throw a heaving line.

Heave taut – To haul in a line until it has a strain upon it.

Irish pennant – The frayed loose end of a line.

Jam – To wedge tight.

Kink – A twist in a rope.

Knot – A twisting, turning, tying, knitting, or entangling of ropes or parts of a rope so as to join two ropes together or make a finished end on a rope, for certain purpose.

Lanyard – A line attached to an article to make it fast.

Lashing – A passing and repassing of a rope so as to confine or fasten together two or more objects; usually in the form of a bunch.

Line – A general term for light rope.

Marlinespike – An iron or steel pin that tapers to a sharp point, used to splice wire rope.

Marry – Temporarily holding two lines together side-by-side or end-to-end.

Part – To break.

Pay out – To slack off on a line, to allow it to run out.

Rigging – A term applied to ship's ropes generally.

Secure – To make fast.

Seize – To bind two ropes together.

Slack – The part of a rope hanging loose; the opposite of taut.

Splice – The joining of two ends of a rope or ropes by so intertwining the strands, as but slightly to increase the diameter of the rope.

Standing part – That part of a line which is secured.

Stopper – A short line, one end of which is secured to a fixed object and used to check or stop a running line.

Strap – A rope ring or sling, made by splicing the two ends of a short piece of rope. Used to handle heavy objects. Small straps used to attach a handybilly to the hauling part of a line.

Take a turn – To pass a line around a cleat or belaying pin to hold on.

Taut – Tight; snug; tightly-drawn; opposite of slack.

Thimble – An iron ring with a groove on the outside for a rope grommet or splice.

Toggle – A small piece of wood or bar of iron inserted in a knot to render it more secure, or to make it more readily unfastened or slipped.

Veer – To allow rope or chain to run out; to slack off.

Blocks are mechanical devices made up of the following parts: a frame (shell) of wood or steel, fitted with one or more sheaves (pulleys); a pin through the frame on which the sheaves rotate, and a strap of manila, wire, rope or steel, fitted around the shell.

Blocks commonly take their names from the number of sheaves, hence, single, double, triple, etc.; or from some special shape or construction. They also may be known according to their use or place they occupy on shipboard.

Cheek blocks are usually placed in fixed positions to perform a specific duty. For example:

The hauling part of lifeboat falls, on the new equipment, runs through cheek blocks which act as fair-leads to the winch.

The size of a block is generally governed by the size of the rope to be used with it. The length of the block should be in inches about three times the circumference of the manila rope to be used, and the sheave diameter should be about two times the circumference of the manila rope. Sizes of small wood shelled blocks such as tail blocks, snatch blocks and blocks used by men in aloft work are often determined by the length of the wood shell. This also applies to small, all-steel shelled blocks as used on handy billies.

TACKLES

A tackle or purchase is an assembly of ropes (falls) and blocks used to multiply power or gain a better lead as in the use of a single whip which facilitates handling light loads but gains no power. If we reverse the single whip and

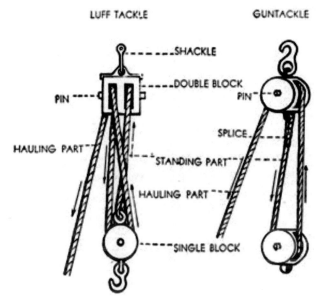

Luff and guntackles.

attach the block to the weight to be moved the applied power is doubled. These two principles can generally be applied to all tackle-stationary blocks give no gain, but serve as a lead to the rope, and all increase of power is derived from movable blocks.

The block having the greatest number of parts of the fall should be attached to the weight to be moved, in order to gain the greatest mechanical advantage. The power gained is equal to the number of parts at the movable block less friction.

Tackles get their name from the number of sheaves in the blocks of which they are composed, thus tackles are designated as twofold, threefold, etc. Tackles are also named from the use to which they are applied, as gangway tackle, guy tackle, etc.

There are many combinations for reeving tackle which are generally based on the type of blocks, number of sheaves and the particular kind of work the tackle is to be used for.

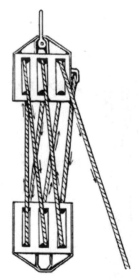

Three-fold purchase tackle.

When speaking of tackle; the following terms are used:

Falls – That part of tackle made up of rope.
Reeve – To pass the rope around the sheaves of the block.
Rove – Past tense of reeve.
Standing part – That part of, the falls made fast to one of the blocks.
Hauling part – The end of the falls to which power is applied.
Overhaul – To separate the two blocks.
Round in – To bring the two blocks together.
Two-blocked – When the two blocks are close together.
Choc-a-block – Same as above.
Handy billy – Small light tackle generally with steel blocks and used for miscellaneous work ship underway.

CHAPTER 2

THE MERCHANT NAVY
AT WAR

The onset of war in 1939 meant that the world's merchant navies had to acquire a new set of competencies extremely quickly if they were to maximise their chances of survival. In particular, they had to perfect the procedures and rules for sailing as part of an escorted convoy, plus train in responses to enemy threats or attacks – by air, mines and by submarine. Prior to the war, the biggest dangers to a merchant ship were periodic storms and, through poor navigation, collisions and grounding. Now the crews had to add enemy aggression on top of those concerns.

In the first extract below, we return to *His Majesty's Merchant Navy*, the first chapter of which raised the important question: 'Combatant or Non-Combatant'. This was a question that, in the early months of the war, would have preyed upon the minds of many a crewmember. During World War I, the U-boat policy against merchant shipping wavered between 'prize rules' – in which the U-boat surfaced, revealed its presence to the target vessel, and allowed the crew and passengers to evacuate before the sinking – and 'unrestricted submarine warfare', where any vessel flying under the enemy flag could be attacked and sunk without prior warning. In World War II, the balance of German tactics tilted quickly towards the latter. The second paragraph of this extract illustrates something of the dilemma for Merchant

Navy crews, in that by taking up weapons against the enemy, even if just for defensive purposes, they dramatically changed their status from civilian to combatant. Yet as the last two paragraphs make clear, the escalating intensity of the U-boat war made any quibbling discussion largely academic – both crews and submariners were in a fight to the death, with little mercy on either side.

His Majesty's Merchant Navy (1940)

Chapter I
Combatant or Non-Combatant?

THE question of whether the merchant seaman is a non-combatant or whether he is to be classed with the Fighting Services is a difficult one to answer. It is particularly so in these days of total warfare when the full fury of a struggle hits warrior and civilian alike.

It is not only just a point for the philosopher to ponder over, because even in these days of semi-barbarism there is a certain amount of adherence to accepted rules even if the adherence is not always rigidly observed by all sides.

For example, it is a generally understood thing that a member of the Fighting Services of any country is, if captured while doing his duty, entitled to be treated as a human being and accorded decent conditions. On the other hand it is equally an accepted idea that a person out of uniform or a civilian who is caught while using a firearm or otherwise taking up arms against an armed man of the enemy's forces, is treated as a *franc-tireur* and thereby liable to be summarily shot. Thus what would be the position if half the crew were members of the R.N.R. and thereby recognised members of a fighting force, while the remainder were civilians? Presumably the latter would be shot and the former accorded the honours of war, if captured.

Certain cases arose out of this in the last war. The ruling then obtaining was that a merchant ship could resist attack but was on no account to open the contest. Thus the attacker always was in a position to get in the first, and probably the fatal, blow. Positions arose where, theoretically speaking, one merchant ship would see a consort torpedoed or shelled and yet, because of the ruling was restrained from hitting back at the enemy. Needless to say, such a position was one in which British seamen would probably act as their own consciences and common dictates of humanity ordered. British merchant seamen very naturally resisted attacks upon their ships and frequently returned the enemy's fire or endeavoured to ram a submarine. If captured the enemy claimed that they were civilians and treated them accordingly.

The passenger liner SS *Athenia*, first UK ship to be sunk by Germany during
World War II.

Now the merchant seaman has in the past always been looked upon as a
civilian, but it is not at all certain that a reversal of this point of view might
not be an advantage all round.

It is recognised that the Merchant Navy is the one most vital service in
peacetime, without which the people of this country would starve. It follows
that in wartime this is doubly true. In fact, the Service is as much a part of the
defence of the Empire as the Fighting Services.

During the last war military decorations were bestowed upon both officers
and men for acts of gallantry or distinguished service. It was accorded the
dignity of an official uniform and its whole status was raised when the King
declared that in future it should be known as the British Merchant Navy
instead of the Merchant Service or Mercantile Marine as hitherto.

Some maintain that *immediately upon the outbreak of a war* it should be
dealt with and regarded as on an equal footing with the other Services. It
would thus, if publicly proclaimed, be entitled to all the honours of war and
its dignity and status more obvious to the country and to the world.

When war broke out in September, 1939, however, it was announced that
in order to maintain the civilian standing of the Service no military decorations
would be awarded but that worthy acts would be rewarded by civilian honours.

This seemed altogether a step in the wrong direction. It had fought for and earned a right to take its place with the armed forces of the Crown.

Arguing purely from the moral point of view it is not at all certain that this civilian standpoint could be logically upheld. If a soldier who fires a gun uses a shell which has been brought to him by a merchant ship, is he more deserving of being termed a fighting man than the other? Again, if a man goes into a shop and purchases a revolver with the express intention of murdering his neighbour and tells the shopkeeper of this, is not the latter just as culpable as the chief actor in the drama? Similarly, taking matters to their logical conclusion, the merchant seaman is going all out to win the war and is not only carrying provisions to the civilian population at home but he is also carrying guns, tanks, munitions and firearms to the troops in the field.

It is a complex problem and people will say that the views just expressed above are those of a totalitarian country; but is this quite fair? For far too long the soldier and sailor have been regarded by most people as hired assassins or at best necessary evils who must be paid for in order to keep the civilian comfortable at home. This is not just. If in modern warfare everyone is striving his best to defeat the enemy, everyone must share the consequences.

This is not condoning the torpedoing of purely passenger ships nor the leaving of seamen to suffer the privations of hours or days in open boats. These things are to be judged by the conscience of humanity, but there must be few who do not at heart admit that as a whole the merchant seaman is a legitimate object of attack. It is the *method* of attack and the total disregard for the dictates of decency that appal one.

After all, in the old days attack on the commerce of a country was legitimate and the merchantmen went armed in consequence. The same thing is taking place to-day.

Would it not be much better to accord the Merchant Navy full Service recognition and thus bring it into line with the remainder of our Defence Forces?

In October, 1939, the German wireless broadcast the following announcement: "Several German submarines have been attacked by British merchant ships in the past few days. Hitherto German submarines have observed international law by always warning merchant ships before attacking them. Now, however, Germany will have to retaliate by regarding every vessel of the British Merchant Navy as a warship."

Perhaps this provides the best answer to the argument.

The Naval Armed Guard (AG) consisted of US Navy personnel assigned to merchant ships, mostly to provide an active defence as gunners, but also to assist with signalling and communications between merchant vessels and Navy craft. The AG was first activated in World War I, to protect US merchant shipping from U-boats. They did their job well, repelling 191 out of 227 attacks, but at the end of the conflict in 1918 the organisation was disbanded.

The case for reactivating the AG rose again in the late 1930s, and although the US Neutrality Act of 1939 prohibited the arming of merchant ships, the Navy began to give informal training in merchant ship defence to numbers of its gunners. On 15 April 1941, however, the AG was officially reactivated, in response to the fact that US vessels were coming under direct threat and attack from German U-boats. Yet it was only with the repeal of the Neutrality Act later in the year that the US Congress, in November 1941, approved both the arming of merchant ships and the deployment of the AG.

The manual *General Instructions for Commanding Officers of Naval Armed Guards on Merchant Ships* was produced in 1944 by the US Navy. It gives a fascinating insight not only into the defensive arrangements aboard merchant ships, but also the human demands of military personnel successfully integrating into what was, after all, a civilian ship.

General Instructions for Commanding Officers of Naval Armed Guards on Merchant Ships (1944)
Chapter I.
The Armed Guard Commander
Section 1.
General

1101. These instructions are for the Commanding Officer of the Naval Armed Guard. In addition to these instructions the Armed Guard officer should refer to and familiarize himself with Wartime Instructions for Merchant Ships.

1102. The Navy Department places its principal trust in the intelligence and initiative of the commander of the Armed Guard. It expects him to foresee and provide for carrying out the details of the difficult and important duties with which the Armed Guard is charged.

1103. The Armed Guard commander represents the Navy Department aboard merchant vessels and Army transports. Whether he be petty officer, chief petty officer, or commissioned officer, his duties are manifold and his responsibilities great.

1104. As commander of the Armed Guard you have been placed in command of a detachment of men of the United States Navy assigned to important detached and dangerous duty. You will be closely associated with officers and men who are not under your command; who may know little of naval customs and traditions. The hearty cooperation of the officers and men of the ship on which you are to serve will be essential to your success. Such cooperation can best be gained by showing toward all officers and men of the Merchant service a uniform courtesy and respect. The Merchant service has its customs and traditions which should receive your respect and observance; inform yourself of these customs and instruct your men in their observance.

1105. Do not forget nor allow your men to forget, that wherever they go, they represent the United States Navy. The Navy Department and the country expect that your conduct will bring credit to the Navy and to the United States.

1106. You must be the leader of your men. Good manners, coolness, and self-control are the first attributes of an officer. You must so control your men as to gain their respect and confidence. Remember it is expected of you to lead, and of them to follow, wherever duty demands, even if death be the result. Be firm; be strict; be fair. Develop the teamwork of your command. Do not fail to use your utmost endeavors and to require equal effort on the part of all your command. Never forget that "good men with poor ships are better than poor men with good ships."

1107. Your success will depend very much on the discipline you maintain in your command. Instruct your men so that they will see the necessity of observing strictly the rules and regulations that you prescribe. Make them realize that the safety of the ship as well as their own lives depends upon the strictest possible performance of duty.

1108. Many of the instructions contained herein are based upon careful study of Voyage Reports and are designed to solve some of the problems confronting the Armed Guard commander insofar as is practicable in General Instructions. Conditions may vary with the many different ships, but if the Armed Guard commander will read these instructions carefully and refer to them when facing difficulties, he will find the solution to many of his problems, or at least information of assistance in solving the problems.

1109. **Armed Guard Bulletins** – The Chief of Naval Operations issues Armed Guard Bulletins from time to time for the information and guidance of the Armed Guard officers. They are designed to be additions to and interpretations of the *General Instructions for Commanding Officers of Naval Armed Guards on Merchant Ships*. Armed Guard officers shall keep their files of Armed Guard Bulletins complete, and upon detachment from the Armed Guard Service, the officer will return his complete file of Armed Guard Bulletins to his Armed Guard Center. In view of the fact that Armed Guard officers' actions are governed according to the *General Instructions* and these Bulletins, it is important that the Armed Guard officer review the *General Instructions* and his Bulletin file at least once a month.

1110. The commander of the Armed Guard attached to a merchant vessel in the Navy Department's representative. He is the master's military adviser and is specifically charged with the vessel's armed defense. He has exclusive control over the military functions of the Armed Guard and is responsible for the execution of all the regulations under which it functions. In accordance with law, the master commands the vessel and is charged with her safe navigation and the safety of all persons on board. The Armed Guard is subject to the orders of the master only in matters pertaining to the general organization of the ship's company. The Armed Guard will not be required to perform any ship duties. Their military duties will be performed invariably under the direction of the commander of the Armed Guard. The master will have been furnished with copies of these instructions and has been directed through proper authority to be governed thereby.

FIRE DISCIPLINE

1111. The following is quoted from the *Ordnance and Gunnery Instructions for Naval Armed Guards on Merchant Ships 1944, Fourth Edition.*

"1301. The decision to open fire is of utmost importance and must be based on two considerations:

(a) The necessity for prompt defensive action.

(b) Safety of friendly units.

1302. The commander of the Armed Guard is responsible for the proper indoctrination of the Armed Guard in fire discipline.

1303. In submarine waters the commander of the Armed Guard may, when not present to exercise control, delegate authority to open fire to the gun captain in charge of the gun, without waiting for orders from the bridge.

1304. In the aircraft danger zone the commander of the Armed Guard will direct gunners on antiaircraft guns to open fire immediately without orders upon any unidentified aircraft which flies within 1,500 yards of the ship, or flies directly toward the ship.

A Naval Armed Guard anti-aircraft gun being fitted to a US merchant ship.

1305. Enemy aircraft will be immediately engaged upon approaching within effective range.

1306. The decision when to open fire is the *responsibility of the Armed Guard commander* since that officer is charged with the defense of the ship. When practicable, however, *without delaying opening fire*, the Armed Guard commander will, in deference to the master of the ship, inform him that fire will be opened.

1307. The commanders of Naval Armed Guards are directed by the Chief of Naval Operations to open fire immediately in the general direction of the attacking submarine even if the attacker is not actually sighted. This authority is delegated to the gun watch by paragraph 1303. The Armed Guard crews are instructed not to abandon ship unless sinking is imminent and gunfire impossible. They are required to take advantage of every opportunity to destroy the enemy by gunfire.

1308. In order to carry out the effective defense of the vessel it is essential that the commander of the Armed Guard and the master of the vessel thoroughly understand their relative responsibilities and authority. The ship must be defended in every means available as long as possible. * * * It is emphasized that the ship's master is by law in full command of the ship, which authority is in no manner restricted by the instructions referred to. The authority to open fire quickly is delegated to the Armed Guard commander by reason of strict military necessity since attacks may develop suddenly by day or by night. There is no situation where either the master or the Armed Guard commander should delay opening fire on the enemy.

1309. The Armed Guard officer is directed to consult with the master on matters of procedure which may vary with circumstances, and which may not be clearly defined in these orders.

1310. Arbitrary conduct and independent actions by the Armed Guard officer in matters where the master has cognizance would tend to lessen respect for the master of the ship, an officer who by law, tradition, and experience, is entitled to certain prerogatives.

1311. Both Armed Guard officers and masters are enjoined to compose personal differences, should any exist, to the end that harmony and concerted action may save the ship and promote the interests of the United States."

1112. The Armed Guard commander is first and primarily a commanding officer, and as such he is charged by Article 1 of the *Articles for the Government of the United States Navy* to show in himself "a good example of virtue, honor, patriotism, and subordination; to be vigilant in inspecting the conduct of all persons who are placed under his command; to guard against and suppress all dissolute and immoral practices, and to correct, according to the laws and regulations of the Navy, all persons who are guilt of them." He should at all times be careful of his person as to dress, speech, and action, so that no person aboard the vessel may have occasion to criticize him for conduct unbecoming an officer. He must at all times remember that the Navy is being judged by him and his conduct. Toward his men he should maintain a uniformly friendly attitude, yet never should he impose undue familiarity upon them nor tolerate undue familiarity on their part. He must set down a discipline for his men and maintain it rigidly and impartially. Petty breaches lead to excesses, intolerable in a military organization. Toward the owners and masters of the vessels he should be uniformly friendly, and, where matters of military security are involved, be courteous, but firmly insistent upon the prompt and efficient prosecution of procedure and action best calculated to protect the ship. Where the rights of his men are in any way jeopardized he must be unyielding in guarding those rights. No greater duty is imposed upon any officer than that of protecting the enlisted men against encroachments upon their rights. The officer whose constant interest in his men has been proved finds his men willing and ready to stand with him until the deck sinks below them.

1113. In many cases, both ashore and afloat, Armed Guard commanders must deal with Army officers of varying ranks. As early understanding of the position of the Armed Guard commander by the Army officers aboard will result in enthusiastic and valuable cooperation. The Army Transport Service is anxious to assist Armed Guard commanders to carry out their duties. Discussion with Army officers aboard merchant vessels will generally result in understanding and cooperative action in the direction of helping the Armed Guard officer and crew in protection of the ship. (Refer to Army Regulations No. 55-330).

1114. In later paragraphs the rights which may be enforced and powers given to the Armed Guard commander will be further elaborated. The basic quality to be exhibited by the Armed Guard commander is Leadership. Leadership requires tact in dealing with men, and with other officers, subordinate and senior. As it is stated in *Naval Leadership*, "Of far greater importance to officers than the material or tools committed to their charge is the personnel with which they are concerned."

1115. **Petty Officers** – As in the fleet, so also in the administration of Armed Guard units, success or failure rests largely with the petty officer. The following is a paraphrased quotation from Naval Leadership:

"Petty Officer means 'small' officer or 'sub-officer.' He is a picked man, chosen because of his possession of certain attributes of character, ability, and experience lacking in his less gifted shipmates. He is capable of assuming responsibility; he is capable of leading and controlling other men; he knows more about his job than do any of those under him. For these reasons he is given the authority to practice his capabilities."

1116. Every effort should be made to impress on the petty officer the importance and responsibility of his position. The average petty officer does not appreciate either his importance or the influence for good or evil that he has in his possession. The importance of the petty officer is well shown in the Navy Regulations which clothe him with full authority to carry on all the duties of his office.

U. S. Navy Regulations, chapter 35, section 1 – Petty Officers, Art. 1275.

"(1) Petty officers shall show in themselves a good example of subordination, courage, zeal, sobriety, neatness, and attention to duty.

(2) They shall aid to the utmost of their ability in maintaining good order, discipline, and all that concerns the efficiency of the command.

(3) for the preservation of good order petty officers are always on duty and are vested with the necessary authority to report and arrest offenders. This authority attaches to them while ashore on liberty.

(4) When an enlisted man is appointed petty officer, the commanding officer shall bring to his attention the provisions of this article."

1117. Again quoting from *Naval Leadership*: "The captain of a ship recognizes the importance and responsibility of the officer or petty officer when, in issuing him an appointment, he says, 'I do strictly charge and require all petty officers and others under my command to be obedient to my orders.' Both afloat and ashore, at sea and in port, in peace and in war, the petty officer occupies a most important position and plays an essential part in the success or failure of his ship. It is often said that 'petty officers are the backbone of the organization on board ship.'"

1118. "Do all you can to draw a distinct line between petty officers and nonrated men. Treat the petty officer with consideration. Let him feel freer to talk to you than the other men, and let him feel that he may do so in a somewhat less formal way. When a petty officer asks a special privilege or liberty, try to grant it. Invite his suggestions and advice. Ask him, when you think it appropriate, how he feels about some matter which should be settled. You need not take his advice, but your evident evaluation of it will make him take a greater interest, and increase his sense of importance and self-respect. Make him feel his superiority over the other men – he is superior, he is a picked man, that's why he is a petty officer. Make the other men realize that to be a petty officer amounts to something; that if they would aspire to the authority and privileges, they must do their work in such a manner as to be considered for rating themselves. Discourage fraternizing between petty officers and their men. Petty officers should never permit nonrated men to address them by their nicknames or Christian names. Let your petty officers know exactly how you feel about this. He owes this to the office he fills.

1119. "Watch you[r] petty officers closely. When they do well tell them so. Do this publicly. Tell them so when they do badly. Do this privately. Instruct them constantly as to your desires, your methods, your general policy. See that they understand thoroughly what you are trying to do and how it is you want them to help you do it. As in all branches of leadership, be consistent in your

A sailor serving in the US Maritime Service.

demands and requirements. Let them know precisely where they stand and what is expected of them. Indoctrinate them."

Discipline

1120. The maintenance of discipline is a vital part of the responsibility of the commanding officer. It is, therefore, necessary that he understands fully his responsibility in the matter, as well as his authority. In connection with disciplinary procedure, it may be necessary from time to time for the commanding officer to assign punishment for infractions of regulations. The assignment of punishment in the Navy is governed by law, and strict adherence to the law is required of all commanding officers. The *Articles for the Government of the United States Navy* in Article 24 outline punishment which may be inflicted by a commanding officer as follows:

1. Reduction of any rating established by himself.
2. Confinement not exceeding 10 days, unless further confinement be necessary, in the case of a prisoner to be tried by court martial.

3. Solitary confinement, on bread and water, not exceeding 5 days.

4. Solitary confinement not exceeding 7 days.

5. Deprivation of liberty on shore.

6. Extra duties.

No other punishment is permitted except by sentence of a court martial and all punishments inflicted by the Armed Guard commander, or by his order, except reprimands, must be entered upon the Armed Guard log, and a report submitted to the Armed Guard center concerned, for entry in the man's service record.

1121. Since it has been determined that the officer in command of an Armed Guard Unit is a commanding officer of a separate and detached command, he has all of the authority and responsibility in regard to the administration of discipline as is given to the commanding officer of any vessel of the Navy. This includes the authority given by Article 28 of *Articles for the Government of the United States Navy* to order summary court martial upon enlisted men in the naval service under his command. And since any officer who is authorized to order a summary court martial may also order a deck court, this authority is also possessed by the commanding officer of an Armed Guard unit. However, in order to try a man by either a summary court martial or a deck court it is necessary to have either a man's complete record or a certified transcript thereof. Since the required records are not carried with the Unit, it is not considered desirable that commanding officers of Armed Guard Units exercise the authority to convene courts martial while aboard a merchant vessel. In more serious cases in which a greater degree of punishment than that which can be inflicted by a commanding officer is determined necessary, the man should be placed on report to the commanding officer of the nearest Armed Guard center and transferred to that activity at the earliest opportunity. If the man's records are not at the nearest Armed Guard center they can be secured by that activity in accordance with current procedure.

1122. Emphasis should be given to the fact that the commanding officer of an Armed Guard Unit has a heavy responsibility and by the same token a high honor. His authority in many respects is equivalent to that of the commanding officer of a combatant ship, because he is in charge of guns and in command of men who fire them. The commanding officer of an Armed Guard Unit and his crew are under the observation of the merchant officers and crew of the vessel under his protection; they are observed by passengers, if any, who happen to be aboard that vessel; they are scrutinized by Army and other Navy personnel if any happen to be aboard. It follows, therefore, that to a large degree the public impression and estimate of naval personnel and efficiency will depend on the example shown by the Armed Guard officer and his crew.

1123. It therefore behooves the commanding officer of an Armed Guard Unit to use the wide authority given him to keep his crew alert, well disciplined, well trained, neat in person, and shipshape in all that the term implies. He must command the respect of his petty officers and men, and keep such control of them that he is conscious every hour of the day and night that he can depend on their readiness for instant, alert, and efficient action.

1124. Such authority can best be exercised by good organization, which means that the commanding officer must work through his petty officer or officers and clothe them with a portion of the authority which resides in him as commanding officer.

1125. Armed Guard commanders should particularly caution their men to observe the following rules while on board ship:

a. Armed Guards shall keep themselves clean, in proper uniform, and shall bear themselves as befits a man-o'-war's man.
b. All unauthorized persons shall be kept clear of guns and ammunition at all times.
c. Drinking wines, beers, or liquors by Armed Guards is strictly prohibited.
d. Gambling by Armed Guards is prohibited.
e. No flame or open light will be allowed on deck at night. Otherwise, it is not necessary that smoking be restricted. It is expected that regulations as regards smoking will be governed as the local situation may dictate.
f. Unnecessary noises or loud talking should not be permitted around sleeping quarters or the navigation bridge. Armed Guards should be especially cautioned to maintain quiet around the Master's and officer's quarters both day and night.
g. Armed Guards should not be permitted on the navigation bridge unless actually on duty.

1126. Gratuities – The Navy Department has been informed that in certain instances foreign governments, their agencies or representatives, commercial firms, or merchant crews have presented gifts of money to naval personnel assigned to Armed Guard duty on merchant vessels.

The acceptance of such gratuities by Naval personnel under any circumstances is considered to be contrary to the customs and traditions of the Naval service.

Hereafter, if any such gratuity is received by a member of the Naval service, it is directed that the gratuity be returned to the donor with a statement that its acceptance is not permitted under existing Navy regulations.

Section 2.
RELATIONS WITH CREW AND PASSENGERS

1201. Limitations of space on merchant vessels necessarily limit Navy personnel available for duty aboard armed merchant vessels. For this reason it is necessary to call upon many duties of the Armed Guard.

1202. It is desirable that all persons aboard a vessel shall be drilled in battle stations so that in time of engagement a minimum of confusion may result, and that persons necessarily engaged in servicing the guns may know their duties.

1203. Where available, it is desirable that military personnel embarked for transportation be utilized to assist the Armed Guard Unit. A request to the senior officer of such military personnel aboard will undoubtedly meet with consent and cooperation. Also members of the merchant crew should be trained and drilled in assisting the Armed Guard Unit. Military personnel which might be available on the outbound voyage might not be available on the homeward voyage, in which event trained members of the merchant crew should be at hand. No one can tell when and to what extent additional trained members of the merchant personnel might be urgently required in manning defensive armament of the vessel for the protection of the ship and themselves.

1204. The following is quoted from Army Regulations, AR 55-330, dated December 1, 1942, for the information of commanding officers of Armed Guard crews on board U. S. Army Transports:

ARMY REGULATIONS
No. 55-330
}
WAR DEPARTMENT
Washington, December 1, 1942.

TRANSPORTATION CORPS
RELATIONSHIP ABOARD TRANSPORTS OF TRANSPORT COMMANDER,
UNIT COMMANDERS, MASTER, AND OTHERS

"* * *.

5. Provision for and status of Armed Guards --

a. Where Navy armed guards are assigned to Army transports their status and the relationship of their commander to the master will be as prescribed in the appropriate Navy Department regulations governing the assignment of Armed Guards to merchant vessels, as amended from time to time. Neither the transport commander nor the Unit commanders aboard will exercise any command over such guards.

b. The transport commander and Unit commanders aboard will, at the request of the master, organize details of troops with machine guns and rifles or other available weapons to stand watch, if necessary, and assist in the defense of the ship when called upon to do so, and will cause such drills and exercises of these details to be held as are required to make them proficient in quickly manning stations and opening an effective fire; but the fire of any such weapons will be at all times under the exclusive control of the person charged by the governing regulations with the control of the fire of the permanent armament aboard. Where the permanent Armed Guard is military personnel this will be the master.

    * * *"

For further information refer to Army Regulations 55-330.

[. . .]

1205. It is important that a thorough look-out be kept at all times for surface and air attack. The officer must insist upon absolute military standing of look-out watches. Failure to stand watches in military fashion shall be a matter of immediate disciplinary action. The ammunition train must be drilled to act quickly, doing a particular job as a reflex action. The prompt servicing of the gun is of vital importance to the successful termination of any engagement. The officer must remember that his guns constitute the sole defense of the vessel upon which he is serving. There is no armor plate or blister to ward off the shells, bombs, or torpedoes of attacking craft. The support of nonmilitary passengers and the merchant crew should be solicited through the master of the vessel. The officer whose efforts and tact fail to bring the necessary cooperation may recall Chapter 4, Section 333, Naval Courts and Boards: "The officers, members of crews, and passengers on board merchant ships of the United States, although not in the naval service of the United States, are, under the laws of the United States, the decisions of the courts, and, by the very necessities of the case, subject to military control while in the actual theater of war."

Section 3.
RELATIONS WITH THE MASTER OF THE VESSEL

1301. The Armed Guard commander must bear in mind that the condition of his battery for firing is but a small part of his duty. He is the military adviser to the master of the vessel and as such his duties are manifold. The Armed Guard commander must realize that the master of the vessel is a man of wide experience and proven judgment in matters of the sea, whereas the Armed Guard commander is generally a man of limited maritime experience. However, the Navy Department recognizing the need for military protection of the vessel, a field in which the master has had little, if any, training and experience, places the Armed Guard Unit aboard as a distinct entity, separate from the ordinary complement of the vessel, in charge of an officer specially trained in the military function. Such responsibilities upon the Armed Guard commanders are not endangered by lack of seagoing experience, for being essentially military in nature, the Armed Guard commander has received the necessary military and naval training, to protect the ship in time of war.

1302. By courtesy, tact, and display of ability the Armed Guard commander must obtain the confidence of the master as a prerequisite to the cooperation between these two officers that is required for the protection of the vessel in time of war. As soon as the master is cognizant of the duties, position and responsibility of the Armed Guard commander, and has gained confidence in him as a man, few difficulties or misunderstandings should arise. It is largely the responsibility of the Armed Guard commander to establish such cordial relationship. In cases where the master absolutely refuses to recognize the sphere of the Armed Guard commander, the problem should be taken up with the port director in a United States port or the naval authority in a foreign port.

1303. Whenever complaints are made by officers of the Merchant Service against members of the Armed Guard, be sure that you conduct a dignified investigation of such complaints, no matter how trivial they may seem. Always inform the master of the result of your investigation. Where punishments are required which cannot be administered by yourself, make a written report to the officer in charge of the Armed Guard center to which your crew is attached. If you are in a United States port, furnish a copy of this report to the port director, or in a foreign port to the naval attaché, and be guided by his advice. Show a copy of such reports to the master of your ship. In all cases arising out of complaints made by the ship's officers, assure both the master and the ship's officers that the Navy will properly punish all offenders. Complaints by unlicensed personnel against members of the Armed Guard must be made through the master.

1304. In cases where food of poor quality or improperly prepared is served to the Armed Guard mess, the Armed Guard officer should take the matter up with the Master of the vessel with the view of making necessary corrections. If the deficiencies are not corrected, the matter should be taken up with the port director or naval authority in the next port of call for assistance in correcting the conditions.

1305. The maintenance of discipline among the merchant crew is the master's responsibility. If he is absent, the responsibility falls on the next senior deck officer on board the ship. This is not the responsibility of the Armed Guard officer.

1306. Naval personnel are placed aboard merchant vessels for military duties only. Armed Guard commanders must not permit their men to be utilized as messengers, deck hands, gangway, or cargo hold watchmen, or the like.

1307. The Armed Guard commander shall detail personnel for sentry duty at the gangway while in ports where such a watch is necessary for the security of the vessel or required by the naval authorities of the port. The sentry will not replace or assume the duties of the ship's gangway watchmen. The duties of the ship's gangway watchmen include tending mooring lines, checking merchant personnel on and off the ship, in some cases searching Merchant Marine personnel, tending boat lines, receiving boats alongside, tending the gangway against movements of the ship, receiving stores and packages, etc. It is the responsibility of the master or merchant officers to provide gangway watchmen.

1308. It is the desire of the Navy Department to instruct and train the officers and men of the merchant crew in all matters pertaining to gunnery and the defense of their vessels. The Armed Guard commanders should make every effort to carry out this training. The training periods should be alternated between mornings and afternoons to enable each watch to attend instruction classes, gun drills, and spotting board practice. The cooperation of the master should be requested by the Armed Guard commander in arranging details of any training which involves Merchant Marine officers or seamen.

1309. Masters and Armed Guard commanders should have a settled plan of action to meet all emergencies. The merchant officer on watch on the bridge should be given instructions by the master accordingly. In formulating these plans, the following should be borne in mind: (1) Weather conditions likely to be encountered; (2) the areas and times in which enemy attacks may be expected; and (3) the types of enemy forces likely to be employed. Particular caution should be exercised during morning and evening twilight.

1310. The master of the vessel shall keep the commander of the Armed Guard informed at all times concerning:

1. The ship's position.
2. The course.
3. Location of mine fields of which the master has knowledge.
4. All war warnings received.
5. Confidential instructions received from Naval authorities as to measures tending to the safety of the ship.
6. The known assistance that may be expected from Allied ships and aircraft.
7. The proximity of a course to the nearest port to which boats may proceed in case the vessel is sunk should be daily determined and responsible personnel informed.

1311. The Armed Guard commander should keep track of the ship's approximate position in order to inform the lifeboat and liferaft crews of the course and approximate distance to land when necessary to abandon ship.

1312. The necessity for **immediate and efficient** action in carrying out prearranged routine the moment an emergency arises or an enemy is sighted cannot be too strongly emphasized. The Armed Guard and merchant crew men should be trained to react practically automatically in an emergency. This means indoctrination, drill, and training. Alert lookouts, quick use of rudder, prompt manning of guns, smooth operation of the established routine, may save your ship and sink the enemy.

1313. In making out the organization every possible detail must be foreseen and covered to the best of your ability. Remember that in organization and provision against submarine attacks there must be close coordination and cooperation between naval and merchant personnel. The commander of the Armed Guard and the master of the vessel should agree upon the procedure for handling the ship and for handling the guns to meet all conditions. It is most important for the master to know how the guns are to be controlled, and for the commander of the Armed Guard to know what the master is going to do when the enemy is sighted. Remember that unless every detail is provided for, covered in drills, and understood by every man on board, confusion will result. In certain waters submarines do not operate. At other times, you are safe from aircraft. In good weather in certain waters you are in danger from both. Confer with the master arranging a flexible, workable system for defense of the vessel depending upon the area in which the vessel is operating.

1314. Take up these questions in succession with the master and come to a working agreement as to exactly what is to be done; then, having decided, make it a daily practice to rehearse by questions and answers with the ship's officers until all are entirely familiar with the plans.

CHAPTER 3
MERCHANT SHIP DEFENCE

The greatest protection a merchant ship possessed was undoubtedly its escort, if available. Escorts packed the heavy weaponry – naval cannon, anti-aircraft guns, depth charges – to engage surface, aerial and underwater attacks, although the levels at which they could tackle those threats varied with the ship types, escort strength and the experience of captain and crew. Much of a merchant ship's defensive capability was largely passive – being vigilant for threats at all times, and taking appropriate evasive actions as early as possible. One notable theme of many of the wartime manuals is that of how to use your eyes, and binoculars, effectively as a look-out. In a vast sky or sea, the look-out would have to discipline himself to scan grey expanses methodically for the tiny wake of a periscope cutting the surface of the water, or a distant aircraft – no more than a spot in the heavens – beginning to line up a bomb run.

Defence could also come from on-board weapons, if provided or installed. In the British Merchant Navy, the Defensively Equipped Merchant Ship (DEMS) programme began in June 1939, upgrading some merchant vessels to receive basic defensive armament. At first, this meant a single submachine gun or machine gun, with an individual sailor given training to use it. Yet as the serious nature of the threat became apparent, more and more ships received heavier weaponry, principally for air defence and for engaging light surface threats such as E-boats or surfaced submarines. The Oerlikon 20mm cannon was a popular fitting; the gun could fire at a cyclical rate of about 320rpm to an effective range of 1,500m (1,640 yds), as was the QF 12pdr 12 cwt 3in naval gun, a single-shot weapon with an effective range out past 10,000m (10,936yds). In 1943 the newer and more powerful Bofors 40mm automatic cannon was introduced on some ships, this taking the full-auto cannon range out to more than 4,000m (4,374 yds).

Manned by Royal Navy or Royal Artillery personnel, these guns could give a good account of themselves against short- and medium-range threats. The merchant ship captain, however, had to be cautious never to think that his vessel had any pretensions to being a warship – evasion was always the ship's best defence.

The first extract in this chapter is from the Admiralty Merchant-Ship Defence Instructions (AMDI) of May 1944. The AMDIs, written throughout the war, were a diverse collection of evolving guidance for merchant crews, providing best practice and new knowledge relating to tactical survival. The note on the cover stated: 'These instructions are to be communicated to D.E.M.S. Officers and Ratings, who should always be permitted to refer to them as requisite.'

AMDI (1944)

INTRODUCTION

PRINCIPLES OF MERCHANT-SHIP DEFENCE

For the successful defence of a merchant ship it is essential to observe the following fundamental principles.

1. **Keep a Good Look Out.**—To fight back you must see your enemy, preferably before he sees you.
2. **Instant readiness to take aggressive action.**—Guns' crews must be closed up and alert, and guns ready, particularly when air attack is likely. Be prepared for the unexpected.
3. **A carefully prepared and tested defence organization.**—Every man must have a duty in the face of the enemy, know how to perform it, and be prepared for any likely eventuality. Organize now. Don't wait till it's too late.
4. **Frequent drill, training and shooting practice.**—Without regular practice and drill, men cannot use their weapons to the best advantage and will be likely to do the wrong thing in the stress of battle. Know your weapons and your instructions.

5. **Efficient Maintenance of the Armament and Defensive Equipment.**—
   If the material isn't efficient, weapons and equipment will fail in action
   when they are most needed. Shortage of ammunition or stores may be fatal.
6. **Appropriate use of Smoke.**—In bad light, smoke and evasive action is
   more likely to be effective than gunfire. Be ready to use it on such occasions.

" Don't be caught napping "

Chapter I
Defence against U-Boats, Raiders and E-Boats
A.M.D.I. 1.—Look-outs—General

1. *Placing of Look-outs.*—Look-outs are a vital part of the defence
   organization of a merchant ship. If a U-boat is sighted before attacking,
   your chances of escape are increased *4 times.*
2. By day in clear weather, a look-out should always be placed aloft with
   the object of sighting and reporting surface vessels or U-boats.
3. In addition to the masthead look-out, all available men, including guns'
   crews, should be employed as look-outs in dangerous areas. The duties

of looking for U-boats and looking for aircraft should be undertaken by different men as the two cannot be combined efficiently. U-boat and aircraft look-outs should be given bearing sectors of a size depending on the number of men available, so as to ensure that a complete all-round look-out is kept.

4. U-boat look-outs should concentrate on the water within a mile of the ship and should look for periscopes and the tracks of approaching torpedoes. In a smooth sea they should also look somewhat further away, as it may be possible to see a periscope two or three miles away if it is travelling fast and making a large "feather." Look-outs should realize that a U-boat may only show her periscope for a few seconds at a time. By night, U-boat lookOuts should be warned to look for U-boats on the surface.

5. Look-outs should be sheltered from the weather as far as practicable, and should be provided with binoculars and anti-glare spectacles. They should be instructed in the correct focusing of binoculars and adjustment of inter-ocular distance in order to reduce eye strain and increase their efficiency.

6. *Reliefs.*—Look-outs should be relieved every hour if possible, but in any case every 2 hours. Men coming up from a lighted compartment at night cannot see properly for a considerable time (about 15 minutes). Look-outs being relieved should not, therefore, leave their posts until their reliefs have become accustomed to the darkness. This also applies to guns' crews.

7. *Importance of Training Look-outs.*—Investigation of U-boat attacks on merchant ships has disclosed that, although in many cases the submarine approached on the surface and was sighted by a member of the crew some minutes before actually firing a torpedo, no report was received by the officer on watch.

8. It is essential that the Officer-of-the-watch should receive immediate reports of the presence of a U-boat. Masters must, therefore, ensure that look-outs are constantly on the alert, know how to report objects sighted, and should seize every possible opportunity of training them in the proper performance of their duties.

A.M.D.I. 2. Placing Extra U-boat Look-outs at Dusk

1. U-boats sometimes shadow ships by day at fairly long range, close rapidly in the failing light after sunset and, either at dusk or shortly after dark, gain a position from which to deliver an attack.

2. A specially good look-out aloft should therefore be kept from just before sunset until dark.

3. It is recommended that shortly before sunset a responsible individual (preferably a junior officer or an apprentice) should relieve or supplement the ordinary look-out and be stationed at the *highest* look-out position in the ship, such as the crow's nest or masthead. He should be provided with the best pair of binoculars available (7 × 50 if possible) and instructed to keep an all-round look-out, but to concentrate mainly on spotting U-boats at medium or long ranges on bearings before the beam.

4. When practicable and where not already provided, ships are strongly recommended to fit a barrel look-out position as high up the foretopmast as possible. This is particularly important in ships that normally proceed independently.

A.M.D.I. 3.—Binoculars for Look-outs

1. Binoculars are supplied by the Admiralty as part of D.E.M.S. equipment and it is now possible to provide two to three pairs for ocean-going vessels and one pair for coasters.

2. These binoculars are intended for the use of Merchant Navy look-outs and the D.E.M.S. look-outs at the guns. They are not intended for ships' officers, except when required by gun control officers during action.

3. Preference should be given to providing available binoculars to U-boat rather than to aircraft look-outs. Due to the small field of vision, aircraft can frequently be picked up more quickly without binoculars, although they are useful for searching a dangerous sector periodically.

4. Binoculars consist of the 6 × 30 prismatic type, and the 7 × 50 type, but there are more of the former in supply. When available. the 7 × 50 type should be allocated to the U-boat look-outs as they are better than the 6 X 30 type, *particularly at night.*

A.M.D.I. 4.—U-Boat Attacks on Independently Routed Ships or Stragglers

1. No merchant vessel should ever tamely surrender to a U-boat but should do her utmost to escape. A vessel which makes a determined attempt to escape has an excellent chance of doing so.

2. *U-boat on Surface—Get your shot in first.*—War experience has confirmed that a U-boat on the surface is particularly vulnerable to gunfire, and

in a gun action with a merchant vessel is generally at a disadvantage. Open fire *immediately* the U-boat is sighted. If within range, sweep the enemy's deck with fire from Oerlikon guns or automatic weapons. This is particularly important in surprise attacks at night or in low visibility and may prevent the enemy from manning his guns, or anyhow cause casualties in the guns' crews. The enemy have attempted these tactics against merchant vessels, so it is imperative *to get in your blow first.*

3. At night, or in poor visibility, the U-boat may present an indistinct target or may only be seen intermittently. Although the chance of hitting is small, it is still desirable to open fire in its direction without delay. Such action may cause the U-boat to submerge and, owing to its slow underwater speed, prevent the attack from being pressed home. If moonlight produces a path down which the escaping ship can move, the U-boat cannot surface astern without offering a good target for the gun's crew.

4. *Smoke Floats.*—At night or in poor visibility smoke floats (or C.S.A. Smoke) will frequently be more effective than gunfire, and under such conditions should generally be used. In addition to making your vessel a difficult target, judicious alterations of course behind a smoke screen will confuse and may shake off a pursuing U-boat, even in broad daylight. Unless baffles are provided for screening sparks, smoke floats should not be burnt on deck at night, but should be dropped overboard.

5. Many ships which have acted energetically on the above lines have escaped, and at least one has sunk or seriously damaged the U-boat by gunfire.

6. *Instant Readiness for Action.*—The degree of readiness for action must depend on the probability of attack. When there is a possibility of attack, the L.A. gun and, at night or in low visibility at least one Oerlikon or automatic gun should always be kept manned and ready to open fire instantly. Remember that guns' crews:—

   (a) must be closed up at the guns, not somewhere about the deck;
   (b) must know their weapons and be able to lay their hands on the ammunition or ignite a smoke float in the dark. Loading practice at night is essential.

A.M.D.I. 5.—Indicating U-boat to Convoy Escorts

1. A U-boat sighted at night should be pointed out to escorts and other vessels by firing short bursts in its direction with tracer

ammunition from Oerlikon guns or other automatic weapons, regardless of range.

2. By day, a round from an L.A. gun should be fired at the estimated range in the direction of the U-boat whether it has dived or not. If, however, the gun will not bear, the direction of the U-boat should be indicated by firing short bursts of tracer ammunition as described above.

3. It is, however, essential to avoid accidental or indiscriminate firing which, besides wasting ammunition, might lead to the position of a convoy being disclosed unnecessarily and would be confusing to the escort vessels.

A.M.D.I. 6.—Immobilisation of Armament if Capture is Imminent

1. Every effort must be made to avoid being captured, but if this seems inevitable the armament must be immobilised otherwise your ship may increase a raider's capacity for further destruction.

2. The armament should be immobilised as follows:—

   (a) B.L. *and Q.F. Guns.*—Remove breach block and throw overboard. If time does not permit of this, throw the lock or striker mechanism overboard, together with spares.

   (b) *Oerlikons.*—Remove and throw barrel, spare barrel or quickly removable parts overboard; also all magazines whether empty or full.

   (c) *Machine Guns.*—For light machine guns, throw the whole gun overboard. For 0.5-in. colts, throw the breech block and spare breech blocks overboard.

   (d) Rocket Weapons.—Bend and damage rocket rails with heavy hammer or crowbar. (A practice shell makes an excellent heavy hammer.)

A.M.D.I. 7.—E-boats-Opening Fire When in Convoy

1. When in convoy on the east coast of the United Kingdom of in the English Channel, fire may be opened at any small craft sighted at night or in conditions of low visibility, which are not recognized as friendly.

2. Under such conditions our own small craft are responsible for avoiding contact with friendly convoys, and those employed in escorting the

convoy will be stationed so that they cannot be mistaken for enemy vessels.

Chapter II
Defence against Aircraft (including Balloons)

"*The Quick and the Dead*"

A.M.D.I. 8.—Rules for Opening Fire on Aircraft—Method of Approach of Friendly Aircraft (T.D. 669/42.)

1. Masters should ensure that defence personnel are trained and practised in aircraft recognition. Every endeavour must be made to recognize approaching aircraft.

2. *At Sea:*—

   (a) Except as directed in sub-paragraphs (*d*) and (*e*) below, merchant ships and fishing vessels at sea are free to engage any aircraft not recognized as friendly which approaches within *1,500 yards.*

   It is vitally important that, once an unidentified aircraft is within this range, there should be no hesitation in opening fire.

(b) Any aircraft clearly recognized by its appearance or actions to be hostile may be engaged by suitable weapons at a greater range than 1,500 yards.

Subject to using only shell set to burst at 1,500 yards or less, fire may be opened on aircraft whilst still outside this range if suspected of being hostile, even though not clearly recognized as such. This will not endanger friendly aircraft, who are instructed not to approach within this range.

(c) Merchant ships and fishing vessels are *not* to open fire with guns or other weapons on *unseen aircraft* (e.g., they are not to open fire on sound or if aircraft is obscured by smoke screen).

(d) In the following areas, merchant ships are not to open fire on aircraft unless actually attacked :—

Atlantic Ocean ..	(i) When westward of 36° West and northward of 25° North, or
	(ii) When southward of 25° North.
Indian Ocean ..	When westward of 80° East and within 500 British or British-occupied territory.
Pacific Ocean ..	(i) When within 200 miles of the North, American Continent.
	(ii) When inside an arc of 1,200 miles radius from Balbao.

Note.—In the above areas, single friendly aircraft may approach merchant ships closer than 1,500 yards for purposes of identification. Aircraft will close by circling and will not fly directly at merchant ships.

(e) When in the North Atlantic westward of 7° West, merchant vessels *in convoy* are not to open fire on aircraft during the hours of darkness unless they are attacked. Merchant ships sailing *in convoy* on the United Kingdom—North American convoy routes are not to open fire on aircraft by *day or night* when westward of 7° West unless they are attacked or the aircraft is proved to be hostile.

(f) Vessels in convoy are not to wait for escorting ships to fire before they themselves open fire.

3. *In Harbour* :—

(a) Anti-aircraft fire from merchant ships and fishing vessels in harbour is governed by the local orders of the port in which they are lying.

These orders will be communicated to the Master on arrival in port by the Naval Authorities.

(b) Subject to the above, any aircraft which is recognized by its appearance or actions to be hostile may be engaged.

(c) British fighter aircraft engaged in operations may not be able to carry out any recognition procedure. H.M. ships and A/A shore defences are warned to withhold fire when fighters are seen or reported to be approaching the defended area. Merchant vessels are to conform to these orders.

(d) It is emphasized that the crew of each gun must recognize an aircraft as hostile before opening fire on it. This is necessary in order that an error in recognition by one gun's crew will not lead to indiscriminate firing by others.

[. . .]

Recognition of Enemy

2. The first essential for timely recognition of aircraft is not necessarily "What sort of plane is it?" but much more "What is the plane doing?" Friendly aircraft are warned that normally they must not approach within 1,500 yards of a British merchant vessel or convoy. Any aircraft that does so should, therefore, immediately be suspect.

3. The fact that an aircraft burns navigation lights or flashes signals or flies low over the ship from the direction of a friendly coast does not necessarily mean that it is friendly.

Readiness

4. In dangerous areas all merchant vessels should be ready to open fire instantly with the whole A/A armament. In a low level attack there will generally be less than 15 seconds between first sighting and bomb-release. Conditions of cloud and visibility may shorten this period.

Note.—Personnel are expected to be organized in two watches for the periods during which ships are in dangerous areas ; any necessary overtime will be paid (*see A.M.D.I. 37*). If the crew too small to provide sufficient numbers in a watch to man all the weapons, priority in manning is to be given to those weapons most capable of dealing with the type of attack expected. (For fuller details *see* B.R.282.)

All-round Look-out and Sectors of Responsibility

5. It is essential that adequate A/A look-outs are posted so that the vessel is not subject to surprise attacks. Unless the enemy is sighted and fire opened before he drops his bombs, the chances of being hit are multiplied 4 times.

6. If warning of the direction of an expected attack is received, the main A/A armament should be trained on that bearing ready to open fire when the aircraft is sighted and within range. It will, however, still be necessary to keep a look-out and have some weapons ready to fire on the disengaged side, in case another attack is made from that direction. The enemy frequently attacks from two different directions at the same time, and also often uses two different forms of attack. For example, a glider bomb attack may take place from one direction when the main and *more dangerous* torpedo attack is being launched from another direction. Similarly, high level bombing may be employed to divert attention from a torpedo bomber or glider bomb attack.

7. Look-outs and guns' crews must realize these possibilities and the defensive organization must include clear-cut instructions regarding the sectors of responsibility for look-outs and also for guns or groups of guns. Guns, or groups of guns, are primarily responsible for engaging targets within range in their own sector of responsibility. When, however, there is only one target within effective range, all weapons that can bear should engage it, but guns, or groups of guns, must continue to maintain a look-out in their own sector of responsibility and be prepared to switch on to any new target that may appear in their sector.

8. If engaging a target outside their own sector of responsibility, one of the ammunition numbers should be detailed to retain a look-out in their own sector.

9. Personnel in charge of guns, or groups of guns, should act on their own initiative in switching their fire on to any new target.

10. A vigilant all-round look-out is particularly important in low visibility, and during dusk and darkness, when attacks develop quickly.

11. Complicated control instruments are not provided and H.A. guns and weapons in D.E.M.S. are not intended for use at high-flying aircraft, when accuracy of bombing is greatly reduced. Generally speaking, two types of weapon are provided :—

(a) Those which are capable of damaging or bringing down aircraft before bomb release, i.e., H.A./L.A. and H.A. guns, heavy and light automatic guns, etc.

(b) Those which should ensure a "kill" if subsequently the aircraft passes directly over the vessel, i.e., wire devices, such as P.A.C. and F.A.M. rockets. Wire devices, besides being lethal, are also a powerful deterrent, and may cause an attacking aircraft to swerve before bomb release and spoil his aim.

Opening Fire (General)

12. Fire must be opened in plenty of time and maintained at the maximum rate of which the guns are capable. On the other hand there is a danger, if fire is opened too soon, of using up all the ready-use ammunition before the aircraft comes within the range at which it may be hit. To avoid this, the control officer, or ratings in charge of the guns, may be given the order to open fire in the permissive sense, i.e., subject to the general rules for opening fire laid down in *A.M.D.Is.* and as described in *paragraphs 15 and 19* below. Indiscriminate firing at enemy aircraft by ships in convoy not only wastes ammunition but, at night or in low visibility, may give away the position and formation of the convoy.

Use of H.A. or L.A. Guns—Barrage Fire

13. As a result of war experience the best all-round fuse settings, which are normally to be used, are as follows:—

1,500 yards ..   For use against both torpedo aircraft and medium or low-level bombers.

500 yards ..   For use against close-range attacks.

Notes.—(i) Under certain special conditions a 3,000-yards fuze setting may be used as a deterrent against high-level and glider-bomb attacks.

(ii) Some shell, whose closest safe fuze setting is greater than 500 yards, will have to be set to the shortest possible safe range.

14. Torpedo aircraft, when attacking, approach in a similar manner to aircraft carrying out low bombing attacks, and the same method of defence is therefore used for dealing with either form of attack.

15. Subject to the general rules for opening fire laid down in A.M.D.I.8 when aircraft are approaching, H.A. or L.A. guns supplied with time-fuze shell should, be used as follows:—

Range at which the aircraft is sighted.	Instructions for Firing.	Fuze setting to be used.
Over 2,000 yards	(1) Open rapid fire with "long" fuze setting as soon as aircraft is estimated to be within 4,000 yards.	1,500 yards. "Long" (L).
	(2) When at 2,000 yards, or as soon as the aircraft is seen to pass through the burst of the "long" setting shell, fire with the "short" setting.	500 yards or closest safe setting with H.E.T.F. "Short" (S).
Under 2,000 yards	Open fire at once with "short" setting.	500 yards or closest safe setting with H.E.T.F. "Short" (S).

Notes.—(i) At night or in low visibility the short setting only is to be used, except in exceptional circumstances where the visibility of an aircraft is over 1 mile, when the normal procedure described above should be used.

(ii) The sights of guns not fitted with A/A sights, e.g., L.A. guns, when used against aircraft, should be set to 1,500 yards and no deflection. There will be no time to alter the setting when attack develops. Deflection should be allowed for by aiming ahead of the target. Open sights should be used at these guns.

(iii) The average speed of attacking aircraft may be considered to be 200 knots, but it is better to over-estimate rather than under-estimate the speed when using cart-wheel sights, particularly at ranges over 1,500 yards.

       (iv) L.A. guns firing H.E.T.F. or shrapnel shell should be used whenever the opportunity occurs against low-flying aircraft.

16. Fuzes must not be set to anything but these two settings. (Except as specially provided for in *A.M.D.Is. 10 and 11* and B.R.282.)

    When the fuzes have been set, shell should be marked in chalk (not paint) with the letters "L" or "S" appropriate to the fuze setting. At the gun position, shell racks or bays in the lockers should be painted "red" for long and "blue" for short, and the shell stowed according to the settings on the fuze, so that they are easily picked out when required.

17. All H.E.T.F. provided for H.A. purposes and shrapnel shell are to be set as follows:—

    (Percentages refer to the total number of H.E.T.F. and shrapnel on board)

    (a) Fifty per cent. of the total are to be set for long range (1,500 yards). Fifty per cent. are to be set for short range (500 yards or the closest safe setting with H.E.T.F.).

    (b) H.E.T.F., if supplied, are to be used for the long setting in preference to shrapnel.

    (c) Fuze No. 400 should be supplied for H.E.T.F. wherever possible, for use with the short setting. With other fuzes, the closest safe setting should be used if greater than 500 yards.

    (d) Where H.E.T.F. or shrapnel shell are supplied with fuzes which cannot safely be set to below 1,000 yards, only one setting is to be used, which should be that indicated in the table for closest safe setting (*see A.M.D.I. 13*).

18. Care is to be taken to ensure that fuzes are properly clamped after setting. Fuze and clamping keys and special screwdrivers will be supplied or should be demanded, to enable D.E.M.S. personnel to re-set fuzes should expenditure necessitate this, in order to keep the correct proportion.

Opening-Fire Ranges (Close Range A/A Weapons)

19. Subject to the rules for opening fire laid down in *A.M.D.I. 8* the ranges at which short range weapons should commence firing are as follows:—

Bofors	1,700 yards
Pillar Boxes..	1,700 yards
Oerlikon	1,000 yards
0.5-in. machine guns	800 yards
0-303-in. or 0.30-in. machine guns ..	400 yards

Notes.—(i) For approaching targets, add 200/300 yards to the above ranges to allow for the targets' movement during the time of flight of the projectile or bullet. Pillar Boxes should only be used against approaching targets.

(ii) Against dive-bombing, fire should be opened as soon as the aircraft starts its dive.

Opening-Fire Range (P.A.Cs., F.A.Ms. and Projectors " J")

20. The following general rules should be observed when firing the P.A.Cs. and F.A.Ms., etc. :—

(a) Against aircraft attacking within their height range, always fire these devices if it appears that the aircraft may pass over the ship or near it.

(b) Endeavour to fire them when the attacking aircraft is at the following distances :—

P.A.Cs. .. ..   500–700 yards
Projectors " J " .. ..   800 yards
F.A.Ms.   .. ..   1,000 yards

(c) If Projectors " J " and F.A.Ms. are linked together and fired by the same switch, endeavour to fire the salvo at 1,000 yards.

21. If no range indicator is available, distances may be judged by fully extending the arm with the index finger pointing at the aircraft. When the wing space of the approaching aircraft is equal to the breadth of the finger, the aircraft will be about 800 yards away.

22. Height range of these devices should be considered to be follows:—

P.A.Cs. ..   ..   600 feet
Projectors "J"   ..   ..   800 feet
F.A.M.s .. ..   2,000 feet

Surprise Attacks (Value of P.A.Cs., etc.)

23. For countering surprise close-range attacks, the most valuable weapon is of the wire-throwing type (P.A.C. or F.A.M.), because it can be fired instantly and does not have to be trained on the target. An officer or man should be specially detailed for control of these weapons both at action and cruising stations.

Eyeshooting Pocket Book

24. The *Eyeshooting Pocket Book* (B.R.254), with which all D.E.M.S. ratings are provided, contains much useful information on A/A fire in general. It should be carefully studied, and read in conjunction with this A.M.D.I.

A.M.D.I. 10.—High-Level Bombing—Extra Long-Range Barrage
General Anti-aircraft Defence

1. The procedure indicated in *A.M.D.I. 9* has proved the best all-round method for engaging enemy aircraft and is to continue to be used under all normal circumstances.

2. In certain areas, however, the enemy have recently attacked and released their bombs from heights outside the normal long-range barrage of 1,500 yards.

3. Without complicated control arrangements, the chances of obtaining hits at ranges greater than 1,500 yards are negligible. It is considered, however, that the use of a longer-range barrage against aircraft attacking from a high level may, if well aimed, act as a deterrent.

4. It is, however, of little use to fire a barrage, even as a deterrent, at very long ranges, and therefore, a 3,000-yard barrage is considered best for the purpose in view. Should the enemy attempt bombing from still greater heights, his chances of obtaining bomb hits will be further reduced.

5. In future, ocean-going vessels proceeding through areas in which high-level bombing (or glider bomb attack, *see A.M.D.I. 11*), may be expected, *e.g.*, on passage from the United Kingdom to Gibraltar, or *vice versa*, or when in the Mediterranean should keep 10 rounds of H.E.T.F. shell for each H.A. and H.A./L.A. gun, set to burst at 3,000 yards, in addition to those normally set to 500 and 1,500 yards.

Procedure

6. If attacked from a high level (4,000 feet or above), the following procedure is to be used:—

   (a) *Open rapid fire* with 3,000 yards "extra long" fuze setting when the aircraft closes to 5,000 yards.

   (b) If aircraft reduces height below 4,000 feet or bursts are seen beyond the target, change at once to the 1,500-yard "long" fuse setting and carry out the procedure given in A.M.D.I. 9.

   (c) *Aim-off* should be greater than normal when using the 3,000-yard barrage, as being of deterrent value only, it is particularly important to burst the shells well in front of the target. Sights should be set at 3,000 yards and 20 per cent. to 25 per cent. be added to the aim-off speed. The speed of bombers at high level can be taken as approximately 150 knots and, therefore, the use of the 200-knot ring with the cartwheel sight is recommended.

L.A. Guns

7. In view of their limited elevation, it will not be possible to use L.A. guns against high-level bombing, but there may be occasions when a 3,000-yard barrage may be useful to break up aircraft formations at low or medium heights preparatory to attack. A few rounds of H.E.T.F. for L.A. guns may, therefore, also be kept set at 3,000 yards for this purpose.

Authority to Open Fire

8. Fire with 3,000-yard "extra long" setting is only to be used :—
    (a) By direct order of the Master, D.E.M.S. Gunnery Officer or Armament Officer (to whom authority may be delegated).
    (b) When there is no doubt that the aircraft is hostile.

Fuze Settings

9. Fuze settings for a 3,000-yard barrage are given in *A.M.D.I. 13*
    Notes.—
    (i) Shrapnel shell is *not* to be used for the 3,000-yard barrage. At this range the velocity of the shell has fallen considerably and the destructive power of shrapnel will be very small.
    (ii) Referring to *A.M.D.I. 9, paragraph 16*, shell set at 3,000 yards should be marked in chalk with an "X" (extra long) and the racks or stowage painted yellow.

[. . .]

A.M.D.I. 11.—Glider Bomb Attacks—Counter Measures

1. Should a glider bomb attack develop the approaching glider should normally be engaged by all possible short-range A/A weapons and also with shrapnel or H.E.T.F. from the larger weapons (*see A.M.D.I. 9),* using the "short" fuze setting.

2. If, however, the controlling aircraft approaches to within 4,000 yards, it should be engaged by the heavier guns, commencing with the "extra long" fuze setting for 3,000 yards on the lines indicated in A.M.D.I. 10 for high-level bombing, with the object of disturbing the control of the glider from the controlling aircraft, Short-range A/A weapons should, however, continue to engage the glider itself. In a recent attack by the direct approach method, both gliders released by an He.177 were shot down by Oerlikons.

[. . .]

A.M.D.I. 14.—Eye shooting—Action Experience

" *Practice makes Perfect* "

1. Do NOT *miss astern.* —War experience has shown that, in action, the most common faults in "eyeshooting" are missing astern and the *failure* to realize how quickly the "aim-off" speed is increasing, and how much allowance must be made for "tracer observations" being behindhand. The man with slow reactions will naturally be the most prone to this *error* because the amount of aim-off required can increase a lot while he is thinking how much it should be. The difficulty of "catching up with the target" if the initial aim-off is too small has shown itself time and again. It is, therefore, best for the initial aim-off to be too large rather than too small.

2. *Aiming practice and dummy runs:*—

   (a) The importance of taking advantage of every opportunity to practise aiming at friendly aircraft (or even seagulls) both at sea and in harbour cannot be too strongly emphasized. *Provided guns are unloaded or at "safe",* guns' crews should not wait to be ordered to

carry out dummy runs, but should do so on their own initiative whenever a suitable target presents itself.
(b) A boxer uses shadow-boxing, amongst other things, as a means of keeping himself in trim. Self-training of ratings is a parallel case; they cannot have too much practice in handling and getting the feel of their weapons. *Footwork*, besides aiming practice, is also most important.
3. *The value of action experience.*—Fire discipline and accuracy of aim are apt to be poor when a ship is attacked for the first time, because in the initial excitement men forget what they have been taught. *There may not be a second time.* It is essential, therefore, that Armament Officers and Senior D.E.M.S. ratings should stimulate the imagination of guns' crews by giving them accounts of what has happened in past actions in other ships. Men who have not been in action before will then have a better idea of what to expect and will be prepared and ready to guard against the more common faults.

A.M.D.I. 108.—Paravanes–General Instructions
1. Enemy-moored mines may be encountered in any part of the world, and paravanes afford protection against mines of this type. Unless used for practice, paravanes cannot be expected to function correctly on service.
2. Unless they have already been used on service, paravanes should be run for half an hour at least once a quarter. This running trial may be carried out in any depth of water greater than 10 fathoms.
3. Whenever paravanes are towed for any purpose, the date and length of time they are run are to be entered in Part II of the *D.E.M.S Defect Book* (*D.E.M.S 15b*) and a note made of any defects that may be observed.
4. The minimum speed at which paravanes should be towed is seven knots. When streaming or recovering paravanes, speech should be no more than eight knots. This will make the work easier and prevent the gear from being subjected to excessive strains.
5. *Maintenance.*–reports of failures indicate that more attention needs to be paid to the proper maintenance of paravanes and paravane-towing gear. These require as much care as any other part of a ship's defensive equipment. It is also essential to exercise cruise in the procedure for getting paravanes in and out.

6. *Correct Assembly of Towing Gear.*–Before running paravanes, the gear must be correctly assembled. The commonest faults are shackling bridles on incorrectly and rigging the paravanes on the wrong sides.

7. To ensure that paravanes tow properly, the span bar and towing rope must be assembled in accordance with the instructions contained in "*Protection of Merchant Ships against Moored Mines*" (O.U. 6299), Plate 5. When the paravane is lying flat on the deck, facing forward, the nuts of the shackle pins should be inboard and on top, the nameplate of the span bar inboard and the roller cutters on the inboard side of the towing wire.

8. *Danger of Tampering with Mechanism of Paravanes.*–Although it is most important that paravanes and paravane gear should be kept well-oiled and greased, it is equally important that no attempt to be made on board ship to tamper with the internal mechanism of paravanes. If paravanes fail to run correctly and the fault cannot be traced to incorrect rigging or defective towing equipment, the fact should be reported to a D.E.M.S. Staff Officer at the first opportunity.

9. *Annual Overhaul.*–Paravanes need overhauling every 12 months. Masters should therefore apply to the nearest D.E.M.S. Officer for their paravanes to be exchanged for overhaul after 11 months on board.

A.M.D.I. 109.–When to Use Paravanes

1. *When proceeding independently* merchant ships are to run paravanes inside the 200 fathom line off any coast, *but only if zigzagging.*

2. The above general instruction is subject to any special directions which may be given to masters with their routeing instructions.

3. *Ships in convoy* will receive instructions for running paravanes from the Commodore.

[. . .]

A.M.D.I. 111.–Paravane Towing Wire–Endurance

1. At high speeds the fatigue limit of paravane-towing wires may be reached before any porcupining or other visible evidence of deterioration appears and, as the cost of the towing wire is small compared with the cost of the paravane, there is no justification for running them to a point at which there is a risk of the wire parting, with consequent loss of the paravane.

2. The following table gives an indication of the probable life of towing wires at various speeds:–

Speed of Ship in knots	Estimated Life of Towing Wire in hours' using		
	18 knot plane	*22 knot plane*	*31 knot plane*
15	67	89	111
17	52	69	86
19	–	55	69
21	–	45	57
23	–	–	47
25	–	–	40
27	–	–	34
29	–	–	30
30	–	–	28

Note.–These figures are for calm weather. When running in conditions of sea worse than 34, the life of a wire should be taken as being only two-thirds of the life of one used in better weather.

[. . .]

A.M.D.I 112.–Maintenance of Paravanes under Arctic Conditions

1. Trouble may be experienced in very cold weather as in North Russia, due to icing up of roller bearings and towing-wire shackles or roller cutters. Unless these parts are free to move, paravanes will not run properly.

2. When low temperatures are experienced, the following precautions should be taken:

   (a) Rudder bearings, towing wire shackles and roller cutters should be well lubricated with the best lowest temperature grease which is on board. Bell's L.T. grease, as supplied for lubricating Oerlikon guns, is suitable for this purpose, but any recognised brand of low-temperature grease will serve.

   (b) Before streaming paravanes it is important to examine the moving parts referred to above; it parts are not free, the best method of freeing them is by means of a steam jet, with subsequent careful driving and the immediate application of low-temperature grease.

The *United States Maritime Service Training Manual: Deck Branch Training* was published in 1943 and became a core training manual for tens of thousands of men entering the Merchant Marine. Its chapter headings reveal the priorities for those employed in the Deck Branch: Steering; Marlinespike Seamanship; Cargo; Ground Tackles and Mooring Lines; Painting Wrinkles; Questions for Deck Seamen; Types of Ships; Submarine Warfare; How to Use your Eyes at Night. The following extract is the chapter on Submarine Warfare, which at this point in the war was by far the greatest threat facing American seamen. The key priority was early detection, if at all possible, through engaged lookouts. As the U-boats often hunted at night, the keenest of eyes were required.

United States Maritime Service Training Manual: Deck Branch Training (1943)

SUBMARINE WARFARE

German submarine *U-210* attempts, unsuccessfully, to escape destruction by the Canadian destroyer HMCS *Assiniboine* on 6 August 1942.

Since the first World War, the German submarine has improved considerably. The modern U-boat is reported to be able to dive to depths in excess of 500 feet and to be impervious to depth charges which would have destroyed her forerunner of 1918. On the surface a submarine presents a small and tough target for gunfire. The rounded surfaces and the thick plating of the pressure hull render the submarine immune to damage from machine guns and other small caliber fire. The conning tower has a very thick plating and has a watertight hatch at its base. Even a penetrating hit on the conning tower will probably fail to destroy the submarine, and it may fail even to interfere with her continued operation.

Damage to the upper part of the pressure hull of a submarine or to the control mechanism for diving prevents a submarine from submerging. If the submarine is unable to dive due to damage, and if she is far from her base and in waters controlled by the enemy, her eventual destruction by hostile air and surface ships is highly probable. A submarine confined to the surface, however, is not entirely defenseless. So long as the submarine retains her ability to use her guns and torpedoes, she is a dangerous vessel. It should be appreciated that not only are guns available to a submarine on the surface but torpedoes likewise can be fired from this as well as from the submerged positions.

A submarine which is undamaged does not normally remain on the surface to use her guns against heavily armed ships or aircraft. By doing so she accepts a needless risk and loses the submarine's greatest asset, the ability to operate submerged and unseen. However, there are circumstances in which gunfire attacks will be made by the submarine. Gun shells are cheaper than torpedoes and there are more on board, as even the largest submarines carry only a limited number of torpedoes-perhaps no more than 32. Also at night a submarine, because of her small silhouette, can approach a large ship and open fire before being seen. She may even destroy her prey before being forced to submerge.

The gun battery of the German submarine consists of one or two guns of three and one-half inches or larger caliber, which would be effective against unarmored ships at ranges up to five miles, and two machine guns which are for attacks close aboard and against exposed personnel. German torpedoes are of two types. One is an air-driven torpedo having an effective range of about eight miles. The other is an electric and wakeless torpedo, which has a much shorter range of two miles. Both types of torpedoes can be fired when the submarine is either on the surface or submerged to periscope depth. Also, they can be fired on sound bearings with the submarine completely submerged to depths of greater than 100 feet.

One or two torpedo hits, if properly placed, will sink a large merchant vessel, although there are many instances of tankers and other ships which have come home after sustaining a torpedo attack from an enemy submarine (upper).

Submarines are equipped with very efficient under-water sound devices which permit them to discover the presence and bearing of large surface vessels within a range of five miles.

This equipment also permits a submerged submarine to keep an accurate track of the position of attacking destroyers and other antisubmarine units. Evasive maneuvers are facilitated by the high maneuverability and the relatively small turning circle of the submarine. The German submarines are reputed to have made considerable progress in reducing the noise of their own machinery, and a submarine proceeding submerged at a speed of less than three knots is very difficult to pick up by even the best and most modern listening gear.

To destroy a modern submarine by means of depth charges the charge must be exploded very near the submarine's hull. To open up that hull a 100-pound depth charge must be exploded within 15 feet from the submarine. The lethal distance is somewhat greater with heavier charges, but in all cases in order to insure a kill the depth charge must be exploded close aboard.

Submarines can proceed on the surface at a speed of 18 knots or better. The submarine carries sufficient fuel to travel around the world. She also carries food and supplies for a cruise of several months' duration. Consequently, the German submarine operating along the American littoral does not need to be refueled or serviced by "mother ships."

There have been press reports that German submarines operating off the Atlantic seaboard have been refueled and have obtained supplies from disguised supply ships. While this is quite possible, the practice is much less general than is indicated by these press reports.

What definitely sends the submarine back home, if she is not sunk or damaged by her enemy, is the expenditure of her torpedoes. When the last bolt has been shot, she must return home to get a new supply. Torpedoes and the human factor determine the endurance of the submarine. This second factor, which may be easily overlooked by even seafaring men who are not accustomed to the cramped quarters of a submarine, is one of considerable importance. Submarine crews are likely to be tough and courageous, but under the continual stress of war conditions, unless frequently relieved and given comparatively long periods of rest and relaxation, their morale may show signs of deterioration. The loss of several famous U-boat captains who were an inspiration to the entire German submarine service has, no doubt, had its effect on the less experienced commanders.

When running submerged, a submarine has a maximum speed of about nine knots. Due to the rapid exhaustion of the storage batteries at this speed, it can be maintained for only an hour or two. At lowest speed, two or three knots, the submarine can continue to cruise submerged for as much as two days, traveling as much as 100 miles during that time. By spending part of the time resting on the bottom, the submarine can remain submerged for as much as 60 hours. Because of the inherent necessity for submarines to surface, preferably at night or in thick weather, to charge their batteries, it is imperative to maintain for a considerable time a close watch on the general area in which the submarine has been seen to dive. This is particularly true when the dive has occurred early in the day. At that time she has obviously less chance of evading her pursuers than when she may be saved by the near approach of nightfall. When it is safe to do so, submarines prefer to remain on the surface, keeping their batteries fully charged for submerged attacks or for submerged escape. To fully recharge an exhausted battery requires about six hours on the surface, but one-half of any battery deficiency can be made up in about one and one-half hours. Usually, therefore, a period of one hour on the surface is enough to recharge batteries sufficiently to permit cruising submerged at slow speed for one day.

In making a daylight torpedo attack on a merchant vessel, the submarine usually approaches submerged, exposing the periscope at frequent intervals, for only a few seconds at each observation. Normally, because of the slow submerged speed of the submarine, the approach upon her target will be made well forward of the merchant ship's beam. The greater the speed of the merchant ship, the farther forward the submarine must be in order to initiate a successful approach. Because the submarine must make frequent and accurate observations and be fine upon the bow in order to be assured of a successful attack, the tactics of zigzag were adopted. This evasive principle frequently thwarts the submarine's plans; and when a zigzag plan has been prescribed, it is highly important that it be followed scrupulously.

Attacks are also frequently made at midnight and 0400, since these are the night hours when watches are in the process of changing, or when the eyes of newly established watch personnel remain unaccustomed to darkness. Since a period of 40 minutes is required to adjust the eye to darkness, this contingency may be avoided by overlapping watch personnel so as to maintain men on lookout who have undergone this adjustment.

Even in good visibility the merchant ship has small chance of seeing the brief exposures of the submarine's periscope or of detecting the submarine by listening devices before the torpedo has been dispatched. If, however, the merchant ship is screened by escort vessels equipped with good listening devices, the submarine must either accept a greater risk of detection or must fire torpedoes at a greater range, and consequently, with a smaller chance of hitting.

It must be borne in mind that the surface speed of the submarine is greater than the speed of all but the fastest of merchant ships. So, by proceeding on the surface outside of gun range, or outside of the visibility range of the merchant vessels, the submarine can frequently redispose herself so as to gain the position ahead to initiate either a submerged approach during good visibility or a surface approach during the hours of darkness. Good air coverage or fast, wide ranging, escort vessels, however, will make it hazardous for the submarine to attempt to overhaul her prey in this fashion.

In making night torpedo attacks, the submarine usually approaches on the surface, relying upon its small silhouette to permit an unseen approach to a firing position. The superior surface speed of the submarine will enable it to maneuver so as to take advantage of any special visibility conditions, such as moonlight, lighter sections of the sky near the horizon, or the glow of shore lights.

In torpedo attacks, either by day or night, the explosion of the torpedo is often the first notice of the ship being attacked. When a torpedo explosion is observed, it may be assumed that the submarine will be within a radius of 5,000 yards of the vessel-roughly on the beam and on the same side as the explosion. As pointed out above, the track of the torpedo is not always visible since many of the modern ones show little or no wake. When the submarine has launched her torpedoes from a shallow depth, the submarine may broach and the white swirl of her propellers become visible.

After firing her torpedoes the submarine ordinarily takes care to avoid exposing herself to gunfire from the damaged ship; remaining out of sight until her prey has foundered or taken such a list that her guns cannot be manned.

In rough weather the submarine will generally dive beam-on to the sea, altering her course if necessary to reach this position. Normally she will surface head-on to the sea. Submarines forced to dive on account of air or surface attacks may alter course after diving. Furthermore, in order to confuse her assailant, a submarine may make a radical change of course just before diving.

There are many reports of the various colors and paint schemes of enemy submarines sighted by merchant marine personnel and other observers. It seems that there is no standardized technique employed. Bearing in mind, however, that the submarine commander is an individualist and usually an officer of considerable resource, it must be assumed that his ingenuity has extended to the point of improvising paints or other protective covering suitable to the area in which he is operating so that his vessel will assume as chameleonlike aspect as possible. On the whole, however, an over-all neutral tone that blends with the seascape is frequently used.

Very often the only proof of an object sighted being a submarine is that it unaccountably disappears. There has been one case during this war of a U-boat disguising herself with sails; a dummy funnel emitting smoke might also be used. There is also the possibility of a hunted U-boat firing a slow-speed torpedo, leaving a trace of oil, which may induce pursuers to follow a false scent.

When attacking unescorted ships in open waters a U-boat will probably endeavor to reach a position well ahead, unseen and on the surface. From here she will gauge her target's mean course. She will then dive fine on the bow, choosing her position from the point of view of light and sea. She will attack at an angle of roughly 90° from the target's course, firing one or more torpedoes at a range of 1,000 yards, or less.

When a convoy has an escort the above method would be risky. It is unlikely that an attack would be made on a single ship with an efficient escort unless that ship is known to be of very great value; but a convoy, so escorted, would probably be shadowed, the U-boat proceeding on the surface hull-down. She would then choose her line of attack so as to avoid contact with the escort as far as possible and would dive at high speed on a closing course.

If possible a U-boat does not fire a torpedo at a single ship when she is more than 1 1/2 points abaft the target's beam. The most dangerous arc is from 60° to 120° from right ahead. When the presence of screening vessels or the target's zigzag interfere with an attack, a U-boat may fire at a range of 1,500 yards and from a position up to two points abaft the beam. When attacking a convoy she might fire a "browning" shot, probably using a salvo of torpedoes, aimed at the convoy as a whole without singling out any particular ship, when the range may be over 4,000 yards.

When attacking single ships, German submarines endeavor, if possible, to close to a range of 500 to 800 yards to fire a torpedo. When attacking a convoy, they fire, if possible, at ranges between 500 to 1,000 yards.

At these ranges the torpedo runs at 35 to 40 knots (depending on the type), i. e., it runs 500 yards in 22 to 26 seconds. It may be expected that longer ranges will be accepted if the target is screened by A/S vessels.

After an attack, one cannot say for certain just what tactics will be adopted. If the target is unescorted they will, as a rule, remain at periscope depth to watch the result of their attack. If an escort is present they will do their utmost to avoid the screening vessels. When the attack has been made at close range it is quite possible that a U-boat may continue diving at high speed and try to remain under a convoy. Normally, however, she will turn off her firing course, dive deep to about 250 feet and proceed at slow speed till the hunt has slackened.

This depends largely on conditions of wind, sea, and light, the number and positions of escorts and whether the target is zigzagging.

In bad weather a periscope is very hard to see, this is partly offset by the fact that the U-boat has to raise a considerable length of periscope to obtain clear vision above the waves. When at long range, as much as 2 feet 6 inches of periscope may be raised to enable details and course of the target to be obtained. As the range decreases the U-boat would show less periscope and, toward the end of the attack, she would possibly only show six inches in calm weather.

In the early stages of an attack a U-boat need not raise her periscope more than once every 5 minutes and then only for 5 to 10 seconds at a time; when nearing the firing position she will raise it every 4 or 5 minutes for not more than 2 seconds at a time.

A periscope cannot as a rule be picked up at a distance of more than 2,000 yards, even with good glasses. If, however, a U-boat is known to be on a certain bearing and weather and light conditions are exceptional, it may be sighted up to 6,000 yards, with glasses.

All modern submarines have two periscopes and a good many have three, but, as a rule, only one of these is used at a time. Only one is fitted for use against aircraft.

At the commencement of an attack a thick periscope with high magnification is used to enable details of the ship and her course to be noted; in the final stages a thin attack-periscope showing a very small "feather" is used.

The number of night attacks, particularly on convoys and stragglers, has now increased considerably. Often a night attack will be carried out on the surface, but the optical qualities of U-boats' periscopes are very good and can be used in twilight and bright moonlight.

In any attack at night a U-boat would be guided by such considerations as position of escort, direction of the moon, and the afterglow of sunset, etc.

She would note carefully the tactics of the escort and run in on an avoiding course at high speed, fire her torpedoes and turn away, remaining on the surface, unless pursued by a fast hunting vessel-in this case she would dive deep and probably reduce to dead slow speed. If she were not hunted she might remain awash and reload her torpedo-tubes in readiness for another attack.

The worst condition for submarine operations is a calm sea, and if, in addition, there is a long swell running, it becomes almost impossible for a submarine to attack unseen.

Merchant vessel dazzle-painted as seen through a submarine periscope.

The same vessel on identical course painted grey.

The visual effects of merchant vessel camouflage.

At the other extreme, if the sea is rough, a submarine will become unmanageable when near the surface. If it is possible for her to make her final approach on a course at right angles to the direction of the sea, she may attack successfully in worse weather; but, unless she is thus favorably situated, she will probably give up any attempt to operate near the surface and will dive deep until the weather moderates.

The principal arc to be searched for U-boats is from right ahead to two points abaft the beam. Any U-boats sighted from right ahead to the bow would probably be at long range so the lookout on that arc should have binoculars if possible. The arcs between 4 and 10 points on either side require the most thorough search as it is there that a periscope or torpedo track is most likely to be sighted. When lookouts are double-banked one man on each side should use binoculars and the other should search for torpedo tracks and periscopes near the ship.

CHAPTER 4

CONVOYS AND ESCORTS

The convoy system was one of the most important naval innovations of both world wars, although its precedents date back centuries earlier (as the second extract below demonstrates). The strength of the convoy system lay in its reduction in the statistical likelihood that an individual ship would be spotted and attacked by a U-boat. It might feel like common sense that a single ship, sailing on its own, had far less chance than a convoy covering hundreds of square metres of being spotted by a U-boat. Yet if multiple ships were sent individually, it was actually easier for a U-boat to find prey; all the commander had to do was patrol the lanes and targets would appear with predictable regularity. By massing many ships in convoy, it was actually easier for the U-boat to miss all these boats in one instance. Of course, if he spotted a convoy, then it was a field day of multiple targets, but the statistical analysis did not lie – ships were safer in convoy. Convoys also had the scale that meant escort vessels could be assigned; a single ship on its own, unless carrying the most valuable of cargo, would not merit an escort.

The *King's Regulations & Admiralty Instructions* quoted below was not a World War II publication – it was actually published just prior to the outbreak of World War I. Yet it is included here because such manuals on the principles and techniques of convoy management would still have been read two decades later. Much of the advice given here, particularly about convoy discipline, would have been just as relevant in the 1940s as it would have been more than 20 years earlier.

King's Regulations & Admiralty Instructions (1913)

Chapter XXX
Convoys

1044. Duties of Convoying Officer. When an officer is ordered to afford convoy and protection to merchant vessels, he is to arrange with the masters of the several vessels such signals as shall enable him to regulate their movements and to learn their wants; he is also to furnish each, on a separate paper, with such secret instructions and signals as he may deem necessary, adding a written charge to each master that he is on no account to communicate the contents to any person, but to keep the paper in his own possession until the end of the voyage, and then, or in the event of his being captured, to destroy it.

2. Information to Admiralty. Before he finally sails from the United Kingdom, he will transmit a complete list of his convoy to the Admiralty; and on his arrival in port with any convoy from abroad, he is also to send to the Admiralty a list in which he is to specify the vessels that arrive with him, and the time and supposed cause of separation of those that do not arrive.

3. Fees, Rewards, &c., from Convoy. He is enjoined not to suffer any person in the ship or ships under his orders to receive, on any pretence whatsoever, any fee, reward, or gratuity from any owner or master of any ship or vessel, or from any person on board, for the protection afforded them.

4. Defence of Convoy. He is to consider the protecting of the convoy as his most particular duty, in the execution of which he is to be very watchful to prevent its being surprised ; he is to defend it if attacked ; and he is to be most careful not to part company from it.

5. Keeping company. He is to keep the merchant ships well collected, and while he will endeavour to proceed with all possible expedition, he will be careful not to proceed at a greater speed than will admit of the slowest ships keeping company with him without risk of straining the ships, or doing injury to their machinery or boilers ; and if any of them shall be in distress, either from badness of weather or other cause, he is to afford them every necessary assistance, which can be rendered without unduly delaying the whole convoy; but if he shall find such distress to be the consequence of the vessel not having been properly fitted or stored for the voyage she was intended to make, he is to report the particulars to the Admiralty.

1045. Disobedience by Convoy. If the master of any merchant ship or other vessel, under convoy, shall disobey the directions given him for his conduct, or by inattention to signals, or by neglecting to keep up a sufficiency of steam, or by any other means, shall retard the progress of the fleet or convoying ships, or shall behave himself disrespectfully to any officer of His Majesty's ships, the Officer Commanding the convoy is to send by the first opportunity a particular account of the same to the Admiralty, specifying the name of the ship and master, and the name and residence of the owner.

1046. Separation from Convoy. If any vessel under convoy shall separate from the fleet without having express permission to do so, the Officer Commanding the convoy is to send by the first opportunity to the Admiralty the name of the vessel and of her master and owner, with the residence of the latter, and also a particular and circumstantial account of the manner, or supposed manner, of her leaving the fleet, and the time of her quitting it, as nearly as can be ascertained, with any other observations with regard to the occurrence he ma be able to offer, so that, if she be afterwards captured, the underwriters may be enabled to judge whether they ought to pay her insurance.

1047. Lights to be carried. The Officer Commanding a convoy may carry one or more lights during the night, as from circumstances he shall think proper; or he may direct any other ship or ships to do so; he will take care, however, that they are not so carried or displayed as to be liable to be mistaken for any established signals.

1048. Convoys in Company. When convoys bound to different ports sail at the same time, or when they meet at sea, they are, for the better protection of the whole, to keep company together so long as their respective courses shall allow; while they continue together the ships-of-war are to carry the appointed signal distinguishing the convoys they belong to; and the merchant vessels of one convoy are to be kept from mixing with those of another, to prevent as much as possible all mistakes and confusion when the convoys separate.

1049. Senior Officer to Command. While two or more convoys continue together, the Senior Officer is to command the whole.

1050. Protection to Vessels of Allies. All officers having the command of convoys are to take under their protection the vessels of His Majesty's allies which shall be ready to sail, and the masters of which shall request it; and they are to protect such vessels as effectually, to all intents and purposes, as those of His Majesty's subjects. But His Majesty's ships are not to take under their protection the vessels of any Power which is at war with any other Power with which His Majesty is not at war, nor the vessels of a neutral Power, unless ordered to do so, or some very particular circumstances shall occur to render it necessary, of which they are to send the earliest possible information to the Admiralty.

1051. Protection to Merchant Vessels Abroad. When the Captain of one of His Majesty's ships is about to sail from any port not in the United Kingdom during war or when war may be expected, if the nature of his orders admit of it, he is to give timely information to merchant vessels, and to take under his protection all those bound the same way, who shall be desirous and ready to accompany him, bearing in mind the directions contained in the preceding Article. Similarly he is to take under his protection such vessels as he may meet with on his passage, if they desire to accompany him, and to see them in safety so far as his course and theirs shall be the same.

In another passage from *His Majesty's Merchant Navy*, Lieutenant-Commander Talbot-Booth sets the convoy system in its historical context, while also explaining its benefits in terms of early actions in World War II. The most perceptive comment he makes, however, is that 'The convoy system is the answer to attack from raiders or submarine, but it is a grave source of danger when there are insufficient escort vessels to protect the convoy.' The lack of escorts for the early years of the war was indeed a significant problem. In fact, until 1941 the merchant ships still made most of their journeys unaccompanied, as escorts often didn't have the range to make full transatlantic crossings. Even an escort, however, couldn't guarantee survival. As an example – one of dozens that could be chosen – the 65 merchant ships and four escort vessels of convoy SC 42 set off from Nova Scotia on 30 August 1941. South of Greenland, it was spotted by an enemy submarine commander, who vectored in a 'Wolf Pack' of 14 U-boats. In a three-day attack, launched mostly at night, 16 ships were sunk and four damaged, with 279 casualties.

His Majesty's Merchant Navy (1940)

An Allied convoy under sail off the coast of North Carolina.

Chapter XXIV
Convoy System

MANY people think that the convoy system was introduced for the first time during the last war, but as a matter of fact it is one of the earliest methods of protecting merchant ships.

As far back as 1379 ships were stationed off the east coast of England for guarding merchant ships from corsairs, and there was an Official known as "Wafter of the Wool Fleet", whose duties appeared to be to keep the wool-laden ships together much as a shepherd guards his sheep.

The Tudor times necessitated every merchantman going armed although, as a matter of fact, in those days there was little or no difference between trading ships and most men-of-war. Privateers and rovers sailed the seas all round the coasts in large numbers, sometimes in whole fleets.

It was during the Napoleonic wars that the really great convoys came into being. Fleets of East Indiamen were rich prizes, and here again nearly all the ships of commerce were themselves armed to enable them to beat off individual attack. It was this that led to the custom of painting imitation gun ports on the hull to bluff the raider into thinking that many weapons were carried, a custom carried into the days of the clipper ships when some owners still kept up the tradition.

Much of the Royal Navy's time was spent in convoying large fleets which sometimes spread out over ten miles or more of sea, and such an assembly was difficult to keep together at the best of times, but when scattered it was a difficult matter for all the bluff-bowed, lumbering craft to gain station again. When the fleet was too heavily guarded the raider would hang astern waiting for stragglers, which he could pick up without much trouble.

Sometimes a tremendous amount of time was occupied in gathering the ships together, and the preparing of the convoy-list giving full details of ships and cargo frequently led to much complaint from merchants.

During these times there were estimated to be about 700 privateers waiting to pounce on the richly-laden merchantmen. During the war with the United States, the American merchants loudly protested to their Government that over 900 of their ships had been lost, and at one time during our wars with France we lost over 800 merchant vessels in two years.

The principal thing which delayed the adoption of the convoy system was the lack of small ships with which adequately to protect them, an old cry which caused Nelson to cry out continually for frigates and yet more frigates.

The other great deterrent was the belief held so firmly in Naval circles, that merchant ships would not be able to keep station in a satisfactory manner owing to their lack of training. When Masters were sounded on this they characteristically replied that if they were told what to do, they would do it.

How well justified is this remark is now a matter of history, because the manner in which the merchant seamen handled their ships became the admiration of the Senior Service. To keep station in peace time even with lights burning is no mean task for officers of warships who are thoroughly trained in the job, but for but for merchant seamen without such previous experience how much more must it be so. They had to learn to zigzag and to carry out every order given by the Commodore of the convoy almost as soon as it was given.

The organisation required ashore is stupendous, but that comes under the Admiralty, and we are here concerned with the Merchant Fleets. In the early part of 1917 the shipping losses were so serious that our plight was becoming desperate, and at one period we were losing ten ships daily, or 10% of all our food ships.

Such was the situation when convoy was adopted in July of that year. Usually they consisted of any number of ships from twelve to thirty. They were formed into three lines, each of which was half a mile distant from the other. There was a quarter of a mile between each ship, and thus a large fleet of some thirty ships would occupy a space of a mile from side to side and 2 1/4 miles from one end of the line to the other. This is shown on the accompanying diagram.

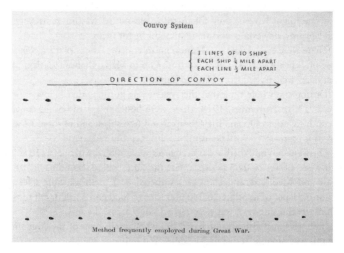

Convoy System

3 LINES OF 10 SHIPS
EACH SHIP ¼ MILE APART
EACH LINE ½ MILE APART

DIRECTION OF CONVOY

Method frequently employed during Great War.

Each was protected by a number of light craft, ranging from armed yachts to trawlers or destroyers. In fact it became a case of using any ship that could carry a gun and which had a good turn of speed to enable her to round up her flock or to dash off and depth charge or attack by gunfire any marauding submarine. In cases where attack from surface raiders might be expected, heavier escort was provided. The whole was under the command of a Commodore who as a general rule flew his flag in one of the merchant ships.

Naturally, a convoy is a slow moving unit as the speed has to be regulated by the fastest possible of the slowest ship, and it is a galling thing to be a member of a convoy whose speed has to be restricted because a few members cannot keep up with the rest. Usually, naturally, convoys are organised of fast, slow or medium ships, but things do not always pan out like this. Another factor against the system is that a certain amount of time has to be lost while ships are being assembled.

Convoys have to be organised so that, perhaps at a certain point of their voyage, one portion breaks off to continue on another course. In foggy weather the ships close up, and usually a barrel or other object is towed astern from each ship so that the disturbance in the water gives some indication to the next astern of the whereabouts of the line.

The usual speed of Atlantic convoys during the Great War was only 8 knots. Vessels of 12 knots or more usually proceeded unescorted, and so did those of a slower speed than 8—they were the lame ducks which had to take what fate might have in store for them; it was no use wasting destroyers on such laggards, however unfortunate it might be for them.

There were two classes of Mediterranean convoys, those of 12 knots and those of 7. From U.K. to Gibraltar, from Gib to Malta, thence to "Alex.", the great fleets were passed from hand to hand.

During the whole time that the system was in force, that is to say from July, 1917, to November, 1918, there were 566 homeward-bound convoys across the Western Ocean. They comprised 8,646 ships, and of these 77 were lost. This represented 0.89 per cent.

Outward-bound North Atlantic figures were 508 convoys of 7,110 ships, with a loss of 45, or 0.63 per cent. For the same period, Scandinavian, East Coast and Mediterranean convoys numbered 85,772 ships, with a loss of 453 or 0.51 per cent. Some 26,000,000 tons of food and 35,000,000 tons of munitions and sinews of war were carried safely across the seas.

In 1918 Great Britain purchased the whole grain crop of the Argentine, and this was brought across in 307 ships, and only one was lost.

Naturally, all the Dominion, British and Allied troops were carried to the various theatres of war under escort, and in 1914 the first convoy of Canadian troops consisted of some 50,000 men, and it was brought across in thirty-four liners at an average speed of 9 knots.

At the outbreak of the present war the convoy system was at once brought into being along lines prepared long beforehand. Once more the chief difficulty of protection was shortage of ships, and many have been guarded by armed merchantmen, which can never be a match for a surface raider.

The first was from Halifax (Nova Scotia), in September, 1939. The Furness liner *Nova Scotia* was flagship, and the escort was provided by two cruisers and four destroyers. A convoy of troop transports is usually a finer sight than one made up of all sorts of ships, as it usually consists of large liners, well known in times of peace but looking strange and vast in their coats of battleship grey.

To the perils of submarine, mine and surface raider of the last war are now added those of ever-increasing aerial attack, magnetic mine, and, in the case of Channel convoys, of running the gauntlet through the Straits of Dover of the many long-range guns set up by the enemy on the coast of occupied France.

The sight of the first convoy to be thus attacked in August, 1940, was an unforgettable one, impressive in the extreme. The sea was choppy and there was a high wind, and the escort was furnished by destroyers of the modern single-funnelled type which continuously doubled back on their tracks while they poured out a dense black smoke-screen to hide their charges which went about their business unhurried and unperturbed.

The Merchant Navy passed by, and when the smoke had cleared and the guns had ceased, the little ships were seen still to be in formation and unharmed, having come unscathed through bombardment and dive-bombing attacks.

Barrage balloons are now used to protect convoys from low-flying attacks, and as the war increases in scope and fury the cry will still go up for ships and still more ships. Convoys naturally vary in size and constitution, but the following list of ships that escaped from the attack on the Atlantic convoy by the German surface raider in November, 1940, may be of interest. They were saved by the gallant action of their escort, H.M. armed liner *Jervis Bay*, which held off the enemy's fire and thus allowed the ships to get clear.

Rangitiki, 16,698 tons; *Cornish City*, 5,492 tons; *St. Gobain*, 9,959 tons (Swedish tanker); *Stureholm*, 4,575 tons (Swedish); *Trefusis*, 5,299 tons; *Puck*, 1,065 tons (Polish); *Sovac*, 6,724 tons; *Erdona*, 6,207 tons; *Empire Penguin, James F. Maguire, Castillian*, 3,067 tons; *Briarwood*, 4,019 tons; *Varoy*, 1,531 tons; *Atheltemplar*, 8,949 tons (tanker); *Lancaster Castle*, 5,172 tons; *Dan-y-Bryn*, 5,117 tons; *Athelempress*, 8,941 tons (tanker); *Oil Reliance*, 5,666 tons (tanker); *Solfonn*, 9,925 tons (Swedish tanker); *Hjalmar Wessel*, 1,742 tons; *Emile Francqui*, 5,859 tons (Belgian); *Persier*, 5,382 tons (Belgian); *Delhi*, 4,571 tons (Swedish); *Anna Bulgari*, 4,603 tons (Greek); *Delphinula*, 8,120 tons (tanker); *Cordelia*, 8,190 tons (tanker); *Pacific Enterprise*, 6,736 tons.

British, allied and neutral, large liner, tanker and tramp all seeking safety together and protected by a former unit of the British Merchant Navy manned largely by merchant seamen.

The convoy system is the answer to attack from raiders or submarine, but it is a grave source of danger when there are insufficient escort vessels to protect the convoy. It is also certain that the ships grouped close together present a good target for attack from the air, and in the present war, at any rate in confined waters, the ships are usually strung out at long intervals and not as shown in the diagram, which was the method described for the last war.

Organisation and Conduct of British Convoys was an Admiralty document, intended to provide proper guidelines regarding the leadership, composition and manoeuvring of a convoy under sail. Explaining these principles with clarity was important, as the convoy would consist of a very varied mix of civilian and military experience, and without proper guidelines chaos could ensue. Note that the overall command of the convoy is placed in hands of the 'Commodore of the Convoy'. He was actually a civilian, but typically one who had previous naval experience as an officer or was serving in the Royal Naval Reserve.

Organisation and Conduct of British Convoys (*c*.1941)

ORGANISATION

1. Escort

The convoy is under the command of the senior officer of the escorting warships, while they are present.

2. Commodore of Convoy

The direct charge of the conduct, manoeuvring and general proceedings of the convoy will be vested in the Commodore of the Convoy who will sail in one of the merchant ships of the convoy and will be responsible to the Senior Officer of the escort for everything appertaining to ships in convoy. In the absence of an escort he will take the entire command.

The Vice-Commodore will take over the duties of the Commodore, should the latter be incapacitated or be absent from the convoy for any reason.

Should both the Commodore and Vice-Commodore be absent from the convoy, the Rear Commodore (who may be the master of a Merchant Ship), or the ship detailed will take full command.

3. Responsibility for Navigation

Masters are always responsible for the safe navigation and handling of their own ships.

4. Cruising Order

Ships in convoy will be in several columns. The ships of each column will normally be in line ahead. A plan of the cruising order of the convoy will be given to each Master before sailing (Form A-1)

5. Distinguishing Numbers

Columns are numbered from 1 to 9, from Port to Starboard. Each ship receives a two-figure distinguishing number. This number is a combination of the column number and of the position of the ship in the column. Example: Ship bearing No. 43 belongs to the fourth column from the port side, and is third ship of her column. Each ship will keep the same distinguishing number, as given at the time of sailing, unless ordered to change by the Commodore.

6. Use of Distinguishing Numbers

Each ship will use her distinguishing number to identify herself when the convoy is forming up or when resuming position after straggling or becoming scattered. When Commodore wishes to give an order to a particular column or ship, his signal will be preceeded by the appropriate distinguishing number. General orders applying to all ships will not be preceeded by any distinguishing number.

7. Guide of Convoy

Unless otherwise ordered, the guide of the convoy will be the Commodore's Ship, flying the Second Substitute (International Code) at the main masthead. When the convoy turns it "gogether" 90° or more to Starboard (or Port), the guide changes, the new guide being the Port (or Starboard) wing ship of the new leading column.

8. Formation of Convoy

When the convoy is forming up, all ships hoist their distinguishing numbers, Commodore Ship hoists the 2nd Substitute. Leading ships of columns place themselves as soon as practicable in their correct position relative to the guide (Form A-1) The ships of each column then form up on the leading ship of their respective column in proper sequence.

9. Distances Signals

Are given on Form A-1 in cables (1/10 mile). Distances between columns are maintained by leading ships of columns. Distances apart of ships in column are from the stem of one ship to the stem of the ship next to her. Ships in column are to preserve their distance (or bearing) from the next ship ahead.

10. Station Keeping

It is imperative for the safety of the convoy that ships in convoy should keep well closed up and that leading ships of columns should not get outside their correct distances. Ships out of station are more liable to torpedo attack, particularly if they drop astern. If ships are out of station, signalling becomes very difficult and slow which endangers the convoy. Large alterations of speed for station keeping should be avoided (maximum ½ knot). When turning use small helm.

11. Changing Station
When a ship drops out of the convoy, the remaining ships of her column are to close up and fill the gap (no change of distinguishing numbers are to be made unless ordered by the Commodore).

12. Procedure in Exchanging Station
When two ships are ordered by the Commodore to exchange station:
    a) if they are in separate columns, the ship in the Port column will always pass astern of the ship in the Starboard column.
    b) if they are in the same column, the advanced ship will haul out of the line to Port, the rear ship to Starboard.
Ships ordered to exchange station are also to exchange their distinguishing numbers.

13. Change of Formation
The Commodore may decide to reduce the front of the convoy and order one of the wing columns to take station astern of the next column. The ships of the column ordered to take station astern of another column are to reduce speed two knots without signal. If the column which has exchanged station is ordered to resume its original position, all ships of the convoy, except ships of the said column will reduce their speed two knots without signal. Normal speed to be resumed when signalled.

14. Beam Bearings from the Guide
When leading ships of columns are ordered to resume beam bearings from the guide:
    a) Ships in the guide's column reduce speed one knot
    b) Ships in columns before the beam of the guide reduce speed two knots.
    c) Ships in column abaft the guide maintain their speed.
    d) Normal speed is resumed when signalled.

15. Station Keeping in Fog
When fog buoys are streamed, ships will keep station on the fog buoy of their next ahead. The best position in which to keep the fog buoy of the ship

immediately ahead, is between the bridge and the stem, about 20 yards away from the ship where it will be clearly visible from the bridge; keep a good lookout in the bows.

CONDUCT OF THE CONVOY

16. Noon Position

Each master will keep his own reckonings. All ships will hoist their noon position (convoy time) daily at 1300, unless otherwise ordered by the Commodore. All ships must take in the Commodore's Noon position, which is the reference position of the day.

17. Time

All times referred to in signals will always be Convoy Time. Clocks will be changed in accordance with Commodore's orders.

18. Courses

Courses and bearings are always TRUE.

19. Rendezvous

Rendezvous for noon two days ahead will usually be signalled by the Commodore immediately after the Noon position. Rendezvous will be given in terms of bearing and distance from Secret positions. Rendezvous are intended only for ships which would lose touch with the convoy, they are not to be used by ships which keep visual contact with the convoy.

20. Zig-Zags

The convoy will use Zig-Zags as ordered by the Commodore. The convoy will usually Zig-Zag by day if weather permits, and also on clear nights. When the executive "Commence Zig-Zag" is made, zig-zag clocks are to be set at once to zero. If the Zig-Zag diagram bears the indication "Reverse and Repeat" after the first hour, it means:– Repeat the previous hour's procedure, but reverse the direction of the turns; turns to Port during the first hour are to become turns to Starboard during the second hour.

21. Lights

Normally all lights are to be extinguished unless otherwise ordered by the Commodore or in emergency.

a) The Main masthead steaming light is to be permanently disconnected.

b) All-round signalling lights are to be permanently disconnected.

c) Navigation lights are to be dimmed to a visibility not exceeding two miles.

d) Rear ships of columns are not to show their stern lights.

However, individual action must be taken by Masters to avoid collision, Lights shown in an emergency must be switched off directly the immediate danger has passed. Shaded stern lights are only to be switched on when necessary to safe navigation.

22. W - T

W/T silence is imperative. In case of enemy attack, the Commodore or the Escort will make all necessary W/T signals. W/T watch is to be kept at the times ordered, and at any additional time that the Commodore may order.

23. Lookouts

It is imperative for a good lookout to be kept at all times and the officer of the watch is responsible that this is done. The officer of the watch should be as free from other duties as circumstances permit. Rear ships should concentrate on a lookout abaft the beam.

24. Funnel Smoke

Is to be reduced to a minimum.

25. Ashes - Refuse

Ashes, wet refuse, etc. are to be thrown overboard and bilges are to be pumped out during the night, between 2100 and 0200. Wooden boxes, wood or floating material are not to be thrown overboard.

26. Damages or Defects

In case of damage or defect, a ship should make appropriate signals to the Commodore. If she falls out of line she should not interfere with the other ships of the convoy. When a ship of the convoy is not under control, she should at once make it known to the other ships by the International signal. A convoy will not wait for a crippled ship.

27. Ship Torpedoed

If destroyers are in company, the ship detailed or in her absence, the rear ship of the column will proceed to assistance. If no local escort is present, no action is to be taken.

28. Smoke Floats
In no circumstances should smoke floats be thrown overboard while in convoy, without definite orders to that effect from the Commodore.

29. Man Overboard
If destroyers are present one of them will pick up the man. If no destroyers are present, no rescue is to be attempted unless ordered by the Commodore.

30. Heaving To
If, on account of heavy weather, the Master thinks it advisable to heave-to, he should not hesitate to ask permission to do so. When the Commodore orders the whole convoy to heave to, the rear ships will heave to first. Ships must open out to a safe distance from each other.

31. Fog or Snow
When in fog the use of the siren is prohibited except in case of immediate danger or for repetition of signals specifically ordered by the Commodore.

General fog procedure:
1. Cease Zig-Zag (on Signal)
2. Resume mean course (on Signal)
3. Stream fog buoy (150 fathoms)
4. Man W/T offices
5. Place cargo cluster over stern.

32. Meeting Local Escort
On meeting Local Escort, all ships are to hoist their distinguishing numbers and to display their name boards in a prominent position. They also are to have ready a line and a float.

ALTERATIONS OF COURSE

33. Alteration of Course By Wheeling
This is the normal method of making small alterations of course when a convoy is in more than one column (less than 40).

a) All ships preserve their relative bearing and distances
b) The guide's column reduces speed one knot.

c) The inner columns (side on which turn is to be made) reduce speed two knots.

d) Outer columns maintain normal speed.

e) Leading ships of all columns adjust their course so as to maintain their distance from the guide, turning finally to new course, and adjusting their speed to the speed of the guide when on their proper bearing from him.

f) All other ships follow in the wake of their next ahead.

g) Normal speed is reduced on signal from the Commodore.

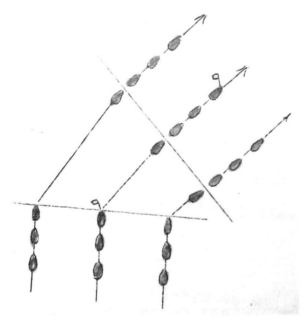

Making an alteration of course by wheeling, the ships maintaining distance and bearing.

34. Alteration of Course Together

All ships alter course simultaneously and the same amount, preserving their compass bearings and distances, but changing their relative bearings.

All ships maintain the normal speed of the convoy.

A convoy of ships makes an alteration of course and formation.

35. Alterations of Course Leading Ships Together

Leading ships of columns alter course simultaneously and the same amount; remaining ships follow in the wake of their next ahead. All ships maintain the normal speed of the convoy.

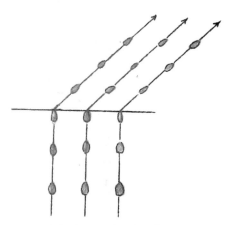

A simultaneous alteration of course.

36. Alterations of Course at Night

a) Anticipated alterations of course at night will be signalled during the preceeding day.

The executive signal for the actual alteration will be made by sound signal: ONE or TWO SHORT BLASTS as appropriate.

Sound signal to be repeated by leading ships of columns.

b) Unexpected alterations of course at night other than Emergency alterations will be made as follows:

(Alteration will always be 20° by wheeling

(Preparatory signal: TWO RED HORIZONTAL lights.

(Executive signal: ONE OR TWO SHORT BLASTS as appropriate.

The turn may be repeated several times by the same signal.

37. Emergency Alterations of Course

By day or by night.

a) The alteration will always be 40° TOGETHER

b) The amount of alteration (40°) is always figured from the course the convoy is steering at the time when the executive is made.

c) Any Zig Zag in progress is automatically cancelled.

d) Preparatory signal 15 SECOND BLAST on the siren.

e) Executive signal:

To turn to Starboard:

(ONE SHORT BLAST

(And Commodore may fire ONE GREEN VERY'S LIGHT

To turn to Port:

(TWO SHORT BLASTS

(And Commodore may fire ONE WHITE VERY'S LIGHT.

Sound signal only, is to be repeated by leading ships of columns.

38. Resume Mean Course and Cease Zig Zag

a) At night Preparatory signal: RED-GREEN-RED VERTICAL lights.

Executive signal: ONE or TWO SHORT BLASTS as appropriate.

Sound signal only is to be repeated by leading ships of columns.

N.B. The above signal will be used in similar manner to COMMENCE ZIG ZAGGING at night.

b) In fog or low visibility Preparatory signal - - . . - -.. (Z Z) on the siren.

Executive signal: ONE or TWO SHORT BLASTS as appropriate.

Executive signal to be repeated by leading ships of columns.

ATTACK ON A CONVOY

39. Submarine

Avoid False alarms – Avoid panic

Any ship of the convoy which sights a submarine close by, or the track of a torpedo, should:

1. Manoeuvre the ship so as to avoid attack or torpedo.
2. If possible fire a gun in the direction of the submarine.
3. If submarine or track of torpedo is sighted on starboard side - HOIST 1 Pendant
   SOUND 6 short blasts.
4. If submarine or track or torpedo is sighted - on port side - HOIST 2 Pendant
   SOUND 2 groups of 6 short blasts.
5. Fire two red socket distress signals or rockets.
6. If time permits hoist a bearing and distance of the submarine.
7. Man W/T Office, but maintain W/T SILENCE

ACTION TO BE TAKEN BY OTHER SHIPS OF CONVOY

1. Convoy will maintain its course and speed and continue any Zig-Zag which may be in force until further orders are issued by the Commodore.
2. If a ship in an outer column is attacked, the other ships in that column may alter course at the discretion of their Masters, but they are to keep clear of the remainder of the convoy.
3. If the ship attacked is damaged and makes no signal, a ship next to her should make the necessary visual or sound signals.
4. Assistance will be rendered within limitations of paragraph 27 (page 4)
5. W/T watch if not already kept should be set at once by all ships, MAINTAIN W/T SILENCE.

40. Surface Vessel

Any ship sighting a suspicious (or enemy) surface vessel is to make appropriate signal at once to the Commodore, giving all possible information re bearing, etc.,..

The convoy will remain together and be manoeuvred by the Commodore while the Ocean Escort deals with the enemy.

In certain circumstances the Commodore may want the convoy to scatter
SCATTER (By day: PENDANT 8
(By night: Series of GREEN and RED VERY'S lights
(By day and by night: — — — .. on siren The signal will be executed as
soon as seen:

    1. Each ship will turn away from the enemy, making sound signals.

    2. Ships of the Commodore's column steer directly away from the enemy.

    3. Other ships diverge from Commodore's column.

    4. All ships increase to maximum speed and man W/T offices.

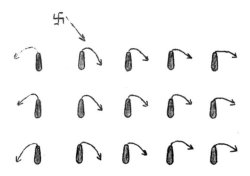

Scattering under a submarine attack.

41. Aircraft

Any ship sighting an aircraft or a formation of aircraft is to make appropriate
signal at once. It is well to remember, however, that considering the distance at
which an aircraft can be seen, it may be impossible to identify their nationality.
All armed ships are to train their guns and be ready to open fire instantly if an
attack materialises.

    It is important that ships should remain well closed up.

    In certain circumstances, the Commodore may want the convoy to
disperse by STARRING. He will then make the following signal:

    STAR (PENDANT 9 – – – . on the siren)

    Execution as soon as seen, as follows:

    1. Ships endeavour to star outwards from the centre of the convoy at full
       speed.

    2. Ships in the van of each column diverge from the mean course.

3. Ships in the rear of each column turn 180° and diverge from the opposite to mean course.
4. Ships in the centre of each column diverge to each beam, approximately 900 from mean course.

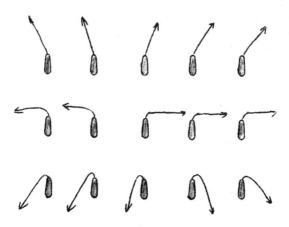

Scattering under an aircraft attack.

These pre-war lecture notes provided an excellent concise summary of the strategies for signalling aboard merchant navy ships. The core methods of visual and auditory signalling would have remained largely unchanged during the war. Radio communications, however, did improve significantly during the war years, giving ship-to-ship transmissions over many hundreds of miles. Yet radio transmissions would invariably have been monitored by German intelligence and could be used to ascertain the position of a convoy. For this reason, radio silence was frequently maintained under operational conditions, or transmissions might be sent in encoded format, although the Germans were adept at breaking these as well.

Lecture on *Visual Signalling for Officers of the Merchant Navy* (1937)

H. M. Signal School,
Portsmouth.
May, 1937.

NAVAL VISUAL SIGNALLING

There are five methods of Visual Signalling used in the Navy:

1. Flags.
2. Flashing.
3. Semaphore.
4. Sound.
5. Fireworks.

Each method has its own particular main uses — Flags for short range signalling in code, replaced by Flashing at night, by an all-round lantern on the mast in peace, and a low power directional lantern in war. Flashing is used for long range signalling with search-lights either in code or plain language. Semaphore is used for short range plain language signalling. The use of Sound Signalling is virtually confined to times of fog when it is not allowed to use Wireless Telegraphy, and, finally, Fireworks are used for alarm and emergency signals.

Details of the procedure in signalling by three methods in Merchant ships are given in the International Code Volume I, but in all cases instructions are only given for signalling between two individual ships and cater only for passing information.

In Naval signalling, this passing of information is required also, but, in addition, we wish to send messages to whole groups of ships which in many cases order a movement or an alteration of course and speed. In time of war, therefore, it is necessary to introduce some form of Naval procedure into international code signalling in order to manoeuvre Merchant ships in company when formed up in a convoy. This procedure entails instructions for repeating signals to ensure all ships addressed receiving the signal and also an executive signal, when it is required for all ships to act on any particular signal at the same moment.

During the late war, a signal book called "The Allied Signal Manual" was issued to Merchant ships. This book contained complete instructions for signalling to convoys, gave details of methods of altering course and speed and contained a code of useful signals. It was supplementary to the International Code and when the latter was rewritten in 1931, it became obsolete and has now been replaced by a new book called the Naval Appendix to the International Code. This book, as its name implies, is supplementary to the International Code with which you are all familiar. It contains all the details required of the procedures I have just mentioned.

This book would be issued to Merchant ships in time of war when so ordered by the Admiralty. Copies are held by the Intelligence Reporting Officers in all ports and these officers would issue the books required. The Naval Appendix is a confidential book and its cover is weighted with lead so that it will sink if lost overboard or the ship sinks.

In this connection, the importance of keeping confidential matter under lock and key cannot be overstressed. In the Navy it is a Court Martial offence to lose a confidential book. It is very important that these books should not fall into improper hands and it is <u>equally</u> important that their loss should be reported immediately it occurs.

There was a case not long ago when a number of confidential books were brought down from the bridge by an officer and put down for a few moments whilst the officer went into the lavatory. He then took them down to lock them up and noticed the absence of one. He thought that another officer must have borrowed it and did nothing more till following morning. The officer who was thought to have borrowed it had no knowledge of it and, after a search, the loss was then reported. Had the loss been reported at once, it is believed that the book could have been recovered before any harm had been done, but owing to the lapse of time, the book had been removed beyond reach.

THE NAVAL APPENDIX TO THE INTERNATIONAL CODE

In order to be able to draft signals and issue signals and issue signal instructions in an unambiguous manner, certain definitions have to be laid down. These definitions are written out in the Naval Appendix, where you find, for instance, that the Commodore of a Convoy is defined as a Naval Officers or Master of a Merchant Ship placed in charge of the Navigation and internal organisation of a convoy. He will sail in one defined as: If ships are in more than one line a convoy is said to be in columns; and so on.

I will now go through briefly the methods of signalling and repeating signals so that all ships in a convoy receive the signal and, if necessary, carry out the signal at the same instant.

We first come to

FLAG SIGNALLING

Should it be desired to send a flag signal to a convoy, it is repeated by ships in the following manner. If the convoy is in single line, the originator hoists the signal close up and all ships in turn repeat the signal at the dip, i.e., about half-way up. The end ship only hoists the answering pendant, there being no need for her to repeat it. When the rear ship understands the signal, she hoists her answering pendant close up; the next ship then hoists the signal close up when she understands it, and so on; and, thus, when the ship next to the originator hoists it close up, he knows all ships understand it. The Executive Signal, that is, the moment it is desired ships to act on the signal hoisted, is the moment when the signal is hauled down and all ships haul down with the originator.

If the convoy is in more than one column, each column carries out the procedure as for single line. Leading ships columns are responsible, however, for the leading ship of the next outer column and they therefore do not hoist their signal close up until the leading ship on her next outer column has hoisted close up.

This can best be shown in a diagram:

```
1.              2.              3.              4.
                Commodore
| At dip       | Close up      | At dip       | At dip
| At dip       | At dip        | At dip       | At dip
| At dip       | At dip        | At dip       | At dip
| At dip       | At dip        | At dip       | At dip
| At dip       | At dip        | At dip       | At dip
```

Explain that leader of No. 1 column hoists close up when he understands the signal and his next astern hoists close up but that the leader of No. 3 column has in addition to wait till the leader of No. 4 goes close up.

SIGNALLING BY FLASHING

Signals made by flashing are made on a light which is directional. The aperture of the light is adjustable and the smallest aperture possible should be used so as to reduce the chances of the convoy being sighted to a minimum.

Signals by flashing are repeated in a very similar manner as signals by flags, each ship passing the signal to her next astern and leaders of columns to leaders of their next outer column. In order, though, that the originator may know when all ships have received the signal, the system of passing in "Z's" is employed. As soon as the last ship in a column has received the signal, she flashes Z to her next ahead and so on; leaders of inner columns do not pass Z to the leader of the next inner column until she has received a Z from her own column and that next outside her.

I will illustrate this with a diagram:

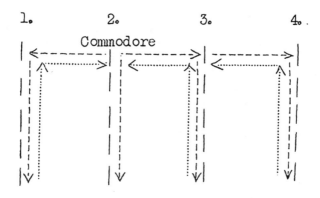

```
------> Signal

·············> Z's
```

Explain that leader of No. 3 does not pass Z to the Commodore until both his next astern and the leader of No. 4 column have passed in Z.

The executive signal in flashing is a 10 seconds flash preceded by the General Call AA and followed by the ending sign . The executive signal is repeated down the lines in the same way as the signal itself but no Z's are passed in. Each ship obeys the signal as soon as she herself has repeated the executive signal.

SIGNALLING BY SOUND
When signalling by sound to two or more ships, all ships repeat the message and therefore no answering is required.

Each ship has a double responsibility:

1. To read and repeat the message correctly.
2. To listen and insure the next ship repeats it correctly.

Sound signals are repeated in a very similar manner to Flashing signals, but care has to be taken not to interfere with others ships. For instance the second ship in the Commodore's columns have repeated it correctly. Z's are passed in as for Flashing but when leaders of columns pass in the Z they follow it with the number of their column.

The executive signal, as before, consists of a ten- second blast preceded by the General Call AA and followed by the ending sign AR. It is only however repeated by leading ships of columns and is obeyed when the last repetition is heard.

SEMAPHORE

Semaphore signals are passed across to leaders of columns and then repeated down each line.

DISTINGUISHING SIGNALS

Now, as you know, when signalling by International Code you can call a ship by her signal letters and other means. These methods are available when signalling to a convoy but normally they are considered to be too cumbersome and also it may be desired to send a signal to the whole of one column. A system of distinguishing signals has therefore been evolved using the numeral pendants of the International Code.

The columns are numbered from port to starboard, the port column being No. 1 column and the next No. 2 and so on. The distinguishing signal of a column is its number preceded by θ (nought) pendant. Ships in the columns are numbered from van to rear, No. 1 being the leading ship in each case. Ships' distinguishing signals are their number in the column preceded by the number of their column, thus the 4th ship in the 2nd column has 24 for distinguishing signal.

This diagram shows the distinguishing signals:

No. <u>1.</u>	<u>2.</u>	<u>3.</u>	<u>4.</u>	<u>5.</u>	<u>6.</u>	Column.
01	02 |	03	04	05	06	
11 |	21 |	31 |	41 |	51 |	61 |	
12 |	22 |	32 |	42 |	52 |	62 |	
13 |	23 |	33 |	43 |	53 |	63 |	
14 |	24 |			54 |	64 |	
15 |					65 |	

These distinguishing signals are used when calling any individual column or any individual ship. If no distinguishing signal is used, then the signal is addressed to all ships present and is called a general signal.

MANOEUVRING A CONVOY

Special signals are provided for manoeuvring a convoy. The principal manoeuvres are alterations of course and speed.

They are peculiar to all other signals and are thus easily recognized. This peculiarity is the position of the Code Pendant. It is hoisted inferior to either S, T, L or K flags.

S flag indicates alter course in succession.

T   ”   ”   ”   ”   together.

L   ”   ”   ”   ”   leaders together, remainder in succession.

K   ”   ”   an alteration in speed.

The amount of the alteration can be signalled in two ways:

1. By hoisting a numeral group of three flags inferior to the alter course signal indicating the new course; thus – T MM 125 – alter course together to 125° true. (Code)

Or

2. By hoisting a numeral group indicating the number of tens of degrees to be altered. If this numeral group is superior, then the turn is to port, and if inferior, to starboard; thus, 4 S MM alter course in succession 40 degrees to port, and L MM 3, alter course leaders together, remainder in succession 30° to starboard. If it is desired to alter the speed of the convoy, the speed desired is indicated by a numeral group inferior to K MM Thus K MM 9 indicates proceed at 9 knots.

The following diagram illustrates how ships act in all cases of alteration of course:

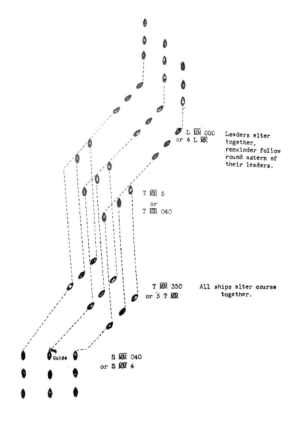

L MM OOO
or 4 L MM

Leaders alter
together,
remainder follow
round astern of
their leaders.

T MM 5
or
T MM 040

T MM 350
or 5 T MM

All ships alter course
together.

S MM 040
or S MM 4

Guide

Guides column reduces one knot, starboard column reduces 2 knots and Leader alters course as necessary to resume his previous relative bearing and distance from the guide, port colum maintains speed and alters course as necessary to resume previous relative bearing and distance from guide.

Convoy resumes original speed by signal.

(Leaders alter together, remainder follow round astern of their leaders.)

(All ships alter course together.)

The only other means of altering course is for use in emergency and in this case the turn is always made together. By the day Commodore hoists the appropriate signal and at the same time sounds a 15-seconds blast on the siren. When he wishes to turn, he sounds one or two short blasts depending on whether the alteration is to starboard or port and these short blasts are the executive signal. The flag signal will probably be kept flying in order to insure all ships seeing it.

At night the turn together is fixed at 40 degrees. The same sound signals are made and at the same time as the short blasts are made, a red Very's light is fired for a turn to port, and a green Very's light for a turn to starboard. This is an example of the fifth method of signalling – Fireworks – which was mentioned at the beginning of the lecture. Another example of the use of Fireworks is the signal to "Scatter". This is indicated by firing a series of red and green Very's lights simultaneously and orders ships to tum 80° as to put the enemy raider astern and disperse the convoy over a wide area.

I hope from what I have said you have understood roughly how the International Code has been adapted for Naval use and for the needs of convoys and escorts. The Naval Appendix also contains detailed instructions for the conduct of a convoy and for the ships in it under headings such as:

Station keeping.
How to act in cases of damage and defects.
Procedure on meeting escorts.
Attack by submarine or surface vessel.

Finally, the Naval Appendix contains, firstly, a code containing useful signals – this code is easily distinguishable as all the groups commence with "Z" – and, secondly, three tables:

1. Single flags for enemy sighting and action signals.
   Example: 6 Pendant – Mine in sight bearing as indicated.

2. Danger and Alarm Signals, which consist of single flags or pendants preceded by the Code Pendant.
Example: Code Pendant F – Gas alarm; on respirators.
3. Surface Craft Reporting Table.

This table gives two groups to be signalled; each group is preceded by the Pilot Jack and consists of five letters. The following information can be signalled: time, day of sighting, nationality, approximate course, approximate speed, type of ship. Code letters are provided for cases when all the above information is not known or cannot be estimated.

SECURITY

As you know, the International Code is in no way confidential and it may be expected in war time that the groups in the Naval Appendix would soon become compromised. It is therefore desirable to provide some form of security when using these two books in wireless signals.

This is achieved by a recoding table. Several editions of this table would be issued and instructions would be given on what dates each table should be used or, conversely, when a new table was to be brought into force and the old one burnt.

This recoding table is merely an organised transposition of Letters and full instructions are given on the cover of each table. By changing the recoding table at fairly short intervals, a high degree security is obtained without the expense of new editions of the books themselves. The recoding table itself is Secret and must therefore be very carefully guarded and if lost, it must immediately be reported so that edition involved may be cancelled and a fresh one brought into force. Naturally this recoding is only necessary for messages sent by wireless telegraphy.

CHAPTER 5

SAFETY AND SURVIVAL

Safety and survival were uppermost considerations amongst a ship's crew in wartime. In peacetime, it was relatively common for safety drills to lapse, lifeboats to be poorly maintained and stripped of their contents, and personnel safety equipment to be lost or misplaced. During the war, such carelessness could have truly lethal consequences. If a ship was torpedoed or holed by an aircraft bomb, the crewmember might literally have minutes to escape the sinking vessel, preferably by lifeboat, and put a safe distance between him and the suction of the ship as it sank. Even if he negotiated the immediate sinking, he then faced the merciless cruelty of survival at sea – rough seas, sharks, hypothermia, sunburn, dehydration, lack of food. In such circumstances, good preparation and proper equipment would often made the difference between having a tale to tell or becoming a loss statistic.

The manuals in this chapter are squarely focused on how to prepare for, and survive, disaster at sea. The first, *Safety for Seamen*, is a fascinating book packed with good advice for the mariner at war. The unnamed author of the book – it was published by the Medical Division, War Shipping Administration-United Seaman's Service – clearly states the quality of his sources in the introduction: 'The inspiration for this booklet came from contact with more than 2,000 seamen who have made use of the War Shipping Administration-United Seaman's Service Rest Centers. Licensed men in the deck, engine and steward's departments, union leaders, oldtimers in shipping companies, doctors with service at sea and men of the merchant services of our Allies have contributed their experiences and ideas. We are also indebted to the Air Force of the Army and to the Navy for their contributions on survival.' The authority of the book shines through in every paragraph, and even has much to recommend it for modern mariners.

Safety for Seamen (c. 1942)

SAFETY FOR SEAMEN

The seafaring man, by choice as well as by tradition, is a rugged individualist. No other industry or profession demands a higher degree of ruggedness. No other has assumed the responsibility for its own individuals to a greater degree.

"Safety" has a very special meaning for the seaman. He faces more hazards than the average, even in peacetime. He has had to look out for himself in home ports, sea lanes and foreign countries.

THE RECORD SHOWS THAT THE SEAMAN HAS HAD MORE ACCIDENTS AND A HIGHER RATE OF CERTAIN DISEASES THAN MEN IN MOST INDUSTRIES. THIS IS NOT NECESSARY AND NEED NOT CONTINUE.

Part of the responsibility lies with others, but to some degree it remains with each man. Improved conditions are essential but not enough. Safety and health also depend on what each man knows and how he acts.

The best possible safety devices will be worthless if you don't know how and when to use them. You may know all about diet but it's what you eat that counts. You won't keep well unless you learn how to prevent disease. If you should get sick, the finest medical care ashore can't help you unless you seek treatment and follow the doctor's advice.

The success of the War of Transportation depends on a small force. The responsibility of each of you to continue to give your best is correspondingly great. It is not necessary to go over the side in order to feel the strain of war. "Convoy fatigue," nervousness, anxiety, inability to sleep, and loss of appetite may occur when men have lived with the probability of attack or have not had enough rest between hazardous voyages. You can learn how to lessen the effect of strain and increase your ability to take it. Men sailing the seven seas are facing the same problems as you are and solving them.

This booklet aims to tell you how. The rules are simple but you have to know them all. You never know which of them you will need. We print them below as your Ten Commandments. The details make up the book.

Merchant Marine 10 Commandments
1. Fight the ship through. Your responsibility—your best bet.
2. Make sure all emergency gear is O.K. Know how to use it.
3. Drill until action is automatic.
4. Take the lead if necessary. Get your bearings plan then act.
5. Keep physically fit.
6. Be expert at first aid.
7. Know how to swim.
8. Learn how to help survivors.
9. Know how to live if castaway.
10. Understand your fears and anger. Learn how to handle them.

I. BEFORE YOU SAIL
GO ON THE SHIP IN THE BEST POSSIBLE HEALTH
In an emergency your life may well depend on your strength and stamina. Too much liquor will lessen it. You may be on short rations for a considerable period and all the strength you store up will come in mighty handy. Ask anyone who's been through it. Get in condition while you are on the beach.
1. Eat a well-balanced diet. That means getting fresh vegetables and fruit twice a day, such foods as meat, fish, poultry or eggs, two or three times a day, two glasses of milk, and as much bread and cereal as you want.

    If you have been drinking get over the effects as quickly as possible. Take plenty of fluids, a good diet, and give yourself three yeast tablets three times a day and a capsule containing all of the vitamins in adequate amounts.
2. Get plenty of rest.
3. Exercise build up your muscular strength.
4. Check up on your physical condition.
5. Get yourself immunized against contagious dieases – yellow fever, cholera, typhus, typhoid-paratyphoid fever, and smallpox. You can save yourself weeks or months of possible severe illness.
6. Take every opportunity to learn first aid, swimming and small boat sailing. These are taught at the Rest Centers and classes can also be arranged through the Port Medical Office at the large sea-ports.
7. If you are over-tired or jittery after a trip, spend a week or two at one of the Rest Centers. It will help to get you in good condition.

Get information at any office of the War Shipping Administration or the United Seamen's Service, or at your union hall.

II. ON THE SHIP
TAKE CARE OF YOURSELF

Eat as well-balanced meals as you can get. Drink plenty of water. If you don't feel well report to the pharmacist's mate or to the officer in charge of the crew's health. Tell him if you are nervous or not sleeping.

SAFETY

Knowledge may save your life. It is the best life preserver you can have and one that you can't lose. It gives you confidence and diminishes fear and anxiety. It is a sign of courage and intelligence to face possibilities and then to figure out what you will do and how you will do it, if they should happen. It's the know how that's all important.

It is natural to be afraid when in danger or when you expect trouble. Remember that the other fellow feels the same way whether he shows it or not. Once you realize your fear you can usually manage it. It often helps to talk it over with the other fellow. If you try to put up a bluff, to yourself especially, you are so preoccupied with covering your fear that you can't think sensibly of what you should do in the emergency.

When men are worried or nervous they are often restless and they are apt to blow their top more than usual. This is natural. It is healthier than keeping feelings inside and then becoming depressed or morose. If you begin to feel that way throw yourself into your job or get a game going and play it hard. If you have a quarrel with a man, put on gloves and slug it out with a referee and rules.

Recreation and relaxation on board ship are important. Divert yourself when not working. Play poker or any other game. Make bets on the day's run. Boxing, wrestling or any sport that will help blow off steam, is a great help.

Officers can organize teams for competitive sports on their own ship and with other ships when in port. Rowing races and other sports will get you in better condition for sailing.

The more your ship's company act together in work and in play the better the spirit and the more reliable and effective each man is. That makes a happy ship and a safer ship.

SAFETY MEETINGS

The more information you have in common, the more confidence you will have in each other and the better you will act together if in danger. Discussions accomplish this. They are particularly important when inexperienced men are aboard but every man can profit from them. The officers and crew may be divided into two off-watch groups. The officers might lead an informal discussion of all the details of damage control, use of equipment, action in emergency, and behavior in lifeboats. The importance of each man and the value of what he does should be emphasized.

One captain held such discussions at each drill. He and the men discussed such questions as when and how to lower the boats under various conditions, getting a full boat if possible, staying fairly near the ship unless there is an explosion, more effective handling of the boat if it is full instead of half empty, etc.

This book can be used as the basis for the meetings. Be sure that each man has a copy. "Wartime Safety Measures for Merchant Seamen," U.S. Coast Guard Series No. 2, will add more detailed information on some of the points discussed.

If the talk about abandoning ship makes you uneasy, remember that lives are saved by knowledge and lost by ignorance. Information and team work, rather than danger, is the point of the discussion.

EACH MAN'S RESPONSIBILITY

When in the danger zone always sleep with your clothes on. Don't sleep on the hatch or sit around on it. Wear long UNDERWEAR that fits loosely. If working in the engine room have it near even in the tropics, as it can be wet and cold at night in a lifeboat.

Fasten to your life jacket or suit a JACK KNIFE with a lanyard attached to a shackle, a WHISTLE, and a LIFE LIGHT. While you are on shore, if possible get a pair of warm long socks, a sweater, long underwear, tobacco or cigarettes if they are necessary to you. Put them in a waterproof bag with a lanyard or wrap them in oil cloth. Small packages of hard fruit candy can come in mighty handy.

A pair of leather GLOVES always kept in a pocket will save the hands from severe damage if you have to go down a rope or tear away hot debris. A HAT may be a life saving precaution against the sun and a pair of dark SUN GLASSES can be invaluable.

If you sleep without your shoes, practice putting them and the life jacket on and getting the waterproof package in the dark until you can do it quickly without fumbling.

KNOW THE WHISTLE SIGNALS.

1. Boat stations 6 short and 1 long blast
2. Lower – 1 short blast
3. Stop lowering – 2 short blasts
4. Dismiss from boats – 3 short blasts

KNOW WHERE YOU ARE. If the captain will post the position of the ship each day, get into the habit of memorizing it and noting the prevailing winds and currents. The U. S. Hydrographic charts are in every life boat.

Work out the course you would set if the ship were lost. On one ship, the captain noted the ship's position at noon each day on pieces of paper and carefully put one in each life boat and raft.

IN ACTION. Figure out beforehand what might happen in any place that you might be in on the ship and figure out what you would be able to do under any of these circumstances. Such brainwork adds greatly to your feeling of self-confidence before a disaster and may save your life during one. You will remember your plan when you need it.

Wear clothes covering the body, as even thin material protects from flash burns. If the ship is being abandoned, put on all of the clothes that you can. Lie flat on the deck pressed hard against a ledge if duties permit when bomb hits are expected. Standing with your head against something solid is the next best. Heavy clothing reduces the shock of a blast.

Keep your head and see that others do. If there is no one in authority around to give orders, size up the situation quickly, take thought, and make decisions for yourself and any others who are not behaving sensibly.

Don't dash headlong for a lifeboat. Make yourself stop for 15 seconds to see whether you have the necessities. Take stock of your situation. This is the best antidote to panic.

LIFEBOATS

The first thing that you demand of a lifeboat is that it keep you afloat; the second, that it take you somewhere. For if no rescue ship shows up, you may be in a bad way if you can't do anything but drift. Every seaman should know how to manage a motor, sail and row boat. A lifeboat, no matter how seaworthy (and be sure that it is), isn't much good if no one can handle it properly.

UPKEEP

Of course, the upkeep of equipment is largely the responsibility of the ship's officers, but they have a lot on their minds under present conditions. Where the interests of so many the very lives of so many are concerned, a few extra eyes to check important details is a real contribution to the general security.

A SAIL OR A MOTOR MUST BE GIVEN ATTENTION PERIODICALLY IF IT IS TO GET YOU PLACES. THE OARS SHOULD BE SEEN TO. If you pay no attention to them until that big moment when they become your principal means of locomotion, you'll be astonished and disappointed at the way they can let you down. Oars should be lashed to rafts so that they can be gotten at in whatever position the raft may float.

Round off the edges of thwarts in the life boat and smooth off any jagged corners of bolts, rivets, etc. It may be your home for some time so you might as well make it as comfortable as possible.

Sails and blankets should be aired regularly so that they will not rot. Wooden masts should be rubbed with oil so that they won't dry out. Stays, halyards, and mainsheet should be replaced when they begin to fray, and turnbuckles should be kept greased so they'll turn freely. ALL TACKLE MUST BE KEPT IN PLACE. Put things back after every drill. Something mislaid may be as bad as something lost.

Keep the PAINTER made fast well forward so that the boat when water-borne rides to the painter and not to the boat fall. The toggles should be well tapered for the quick release of the sea painter, and it and the mousing hooks painted white or luminous.

After any action the lifeboats and rafts should be gone over for any damage. For damage after launching, REPAIR KITS are provided in each boat and every man should know how to use them. See that the bag of 25 BULLET HOLE PLUGS is properly secured so that it won't float away. A BUCKET OF SAND near the lifeboats will come in handy if oil is thrown up by explosives.

BOAT COVERS are necessary on tankers, but on dry cargo vessels, unless there is snow and ice, they should be stowed in the boat.

Wet the inside landing edges of boat planks every day in hot weather by playing the hose around the inside of the gunnel on the side benching. Drain away the water and replace the plug. There should be two plugs.

EQUIPMENT IN THE LIFEBOAT

Each contains a liquid compass, (the liquid is a poison), four day time distress signals and one or two distress lights, 3 drinking cups, a first aid kit, and a ditty bag with sailmaker's palm needles, twine, marline and marlinspike.

A SEA-ANCHOR is required in each lifeboat.

See that there is a gallon of VEGETABLE OR ANIMAL OIL aboard. The container should be so arranged that it can be attached to the sea-anchor. Be sure to remember to use it when sailing the boat in a heavy sea.

WIRE STRETCHERS are recommended to lower injured persons into a lifeboat.

SIGNALLING MIRRORS are required to be in every lifeboat and raft. Flashes from them can be seen as far as 10 miles on a clear day. Continuous rapid flashes can be seen in a plane flying too high to see the lifeboat or raft.

One PORTABLE RADIO is required to be available and readily accessible for use in lifeboats or a radio installation in at least one lifeboat on each side of the ship.

Keep the FLASHLIGHT in a place which everyone knows so that it can be found at night. It will help locate men in the water.

Two EXTRA LIFE PRESERVERS are in each lifeboat. A manila line should be attached to be used as a heaving line to throw the life preserver to men struggling in the water.

See that all deck equipment is lashed securely so that it will not get in the way if the ship is struck. Be sure that everything is securely lashed in the lifeboat. Also, every member of the crew should know how to release the lifeboat. The releasing gear should be painted white or luminous.

PROVISIONS

It is the officers' duty to check the water and other provisions at each boat drill, particularly to be sure that the water containers are full. The water should be changed every two weeks. See that the bungs are securely fastened with leather or canvas strap.

Since water is more important than food, as much water as possible should be taken along. Oil drums can be cleaned and sterilized by steam in the engine room and half filled with drinking water. They should be painted white, provided with rings or lashing and stored on the upper deck so that they can be rolled off and later lashed to the boat or raft.

If there is time, get a sack of potatoes, onions or turnips. They contain water and necessary food elements. In lifeboats with floors, condensed milk, canned tomatoes and fruit juices can be stored under the floor and are of great value.

NEW EQUIPMENT to increase safety has been developed and new ideas are being tested. This includes exposure suits, protection against sun, devices to take the salt out of sea water, rations that will best maintain strength and improved signalling devices. The value of any gear depends on the knowledge and coolness of the men using it.

DRILL

Drill until every action is automatic and the purpose and use of safety equipment is thoroughly understood. Drill must be held not less than once in four days. The best equipment is worthless unless you know how to use it quickly and accurately. Every man should be told patiently and in detail just what is expected of him. This should be repeated until he can do it speedily and without having to think about it or get in another man's way. Nothing increases the confidence of men more than the efficiency of drills and of the officers who conduct them.

In addition, every man should know every job that has to be done in lifeboat or on a raft. His life may depend on it. The other men may be helpless or he may be alone.

[. . .]

SUCTION

There is a legend that every vessel has a tremendous suction that draws everything down within a radius of a hundred yards, like some terrifying miniature maelstrom. This is definitely an exaggeration. It is true that if a ship is really sinking it's a good idea to get perhaps 30 feet from her. But there is more danger from too great hurry and panic in getting away than from suction.

We know of a case in which a ship sank under several men in seven minutes and not one of them was dragged under. Naturally, if you are near some large opening like a main hatch or a smoke pipe, the water will rush in, dragging everything afloat including you with it. But even so, unless you get trapped, you will float out before you drown, or may even be pushed out by the escaping air.

If you are some distance from hatches and funnels, the chances are that you can almost certainly walk off safely, if you have to stay that long to do your job right.

GETTING OFF ON YOUR OWN

If you cannot go over the side in a life boat, take a good look at the situation,

1. Have on a life jacket,
2. Get over the side on a cargo net, Jacob's ladder or line. Lower yourself rather than jump.
3. If there are none of these, look for a fire hose. It offers a better grasp than a rope, but look out for the nozzle. Make sure that it has been belayed.

    Gloves will keep you from cutting your hands, or slipping if the hose or rope is covered with oil. Always go hand over hand on hose or rope.

    NEVER SLIDE. If there is a man above you and he slides, keep well braced and have your head to one side. Take his weight on your shoulders. Do not let go of the rope until your feet are in the water.
4. JUMP AS A LAST RESORT ONLY if there is no other means of leaving the ship. Go over the weather side near the bow or near the stern if the propeller is stopped and the stern is lower. If possible do not go over the lee side. If the ship is drifting fast you may be trapped against the side or by loose cargo in the water.

Look for a place to jump that is fairly free from oil and debris and nearer to a lifeboat, raft or other swimmers. If you have a life jacket keep your shoes on.

In jumping, cross the arms over the front of the life jacket. With one hand on your shoulder hold the kapok jacket down so that it won't get over your head when you hit the water. Keep your legs together when you jump so that you won't hurt yourself severely. Hold your nose.

Jump as far out from the ship as possible.

If you wear a cork life jacket it is even more important to cross the arms and hold the jacket down firmly at the shoulders with the hands. Otherwise it can ride up when you hit the water, throw your head back and break your neck.

Get under way smartly on the course marked out in your mind so as to be out of the way of falling debris or explosives. Once out of these dangers, slow down and swim toward your goal. You have more chance to be seen and picked up in a group. Don't climb on a raft if there are a number of people on it – it may submerge. Hang on to it.

Flash your life jacket light on and off quickly so that at least some of the flashes occur when you are at the crest of a wave.

If you have no life jacket or suit any floating debris will help you stay up. You can sometimes get a better grip if you jab your jack-knife into the wood.

You can tread water, take off your pants or jacket, tie a knot in the legs or sleeves, button them up and swing them through the air so that the arms and legs fill with air. Then twist the open ends so that the air stays in and you have a life preserver. Lie on your back and float.

Don't thrash about or swim uselessly. Slow relaxed strokes made with the arms moving like the oars of a boat when being rowed, and a slow kick help keep a man up if he has no life jacket. Every seaman should know how to swim.

If you see sharks make a commotion in the water to scare them and have your knife ready. Yelling alarms other survivors already wrought up and doesn't scare the shark.

If depth charges are going off around you, you may possibly avoid injury by lowering your life jacket to cover the small of your back and belly and as much of the chest as possible. Swim on your back, keeping as much of your body out of water as you can.

SAFETY FOR TANKERMEN

KNOW THE JOB. On tankers, barring a direct hit, panic is a greater danger than the enemy. Since fire is the most serious hazard, have a bucket of water in all crew's quarters to wet clothes and towels to wrap around the head, face and hands in escaping through flames. This could apply to all ships in danger zones.

If possible a tanker lifeboat should carry only half of its capacity as it is difficult to manoeuver in oil slick. Every tankerman should know every boat job because some men may not reach their stations. Men in the steward's department and engine room should have special training in lifeboat handling. There should be at least four men to a boat if possible fewer than that would find it difficult to handle.

The life lines fastened to the ship should be lowered before the falls are paid out so that they won't foul on the men in the boat and yank them over the side.

If the painter is not fire-proofed use 30 feet of wire with a manila tail leading into the boat. A steering oar is better than a rudder in getting away through oil slick. A navy type steering oar and lock or becket is best as the usual type would have to be lashed. Paint the blade white so that it can be picked out at night.

Life rafts are useless for tankers except under the most favorable conditions, as they cannot be controlled. If they are used, launch them as near as possible to lifeboats so that a line can be passed from the raft to the boat. Set the boat to windward as soon as possible and watch that the wind doesn't change.

SWIMMING IN OIL. If, as a last resort, you must go over the side into oil slick or flames, first take off your life preserver because you must swim underwater. Swimming in oil is like swimming through mud. Wait for a clear spot, gauge the distance, be sure that you are facing to windward, then jump feet first. Swim under water. On coming up for air through the oil, turn around so that your face is against the wind, pushing the water and oil away from you with short strokes. Breathe and submerge and swim again to windward. The Navy film MG-2063 "How to Swim through Burning Oil and through Surf" can be seen in the Rest Centers or borrowed for showing in union halls, U.S.S. recreation centers and hotels.

There is nothing equivocal about the title *How to Abandon Ship*. It was published in 1943, written by mariners Phil Richards and John J. Branigan. Like *Safety at Sea* above, *How to Abandon Ship* was produced with extensive research amongst sailors who had endured the worst. The introduction states: 'To scores of seamen from torpedoed ships, the authors pay humble tribute for their generous aid in the preparation of this manual.' Branigan himself had been serving as Third Officer on the SS *Robin Moor* when it was sunk by a U-boat on 21 May 1941, making it the first US merchant vessel to be sunk by the Germans in the war. First-hand experience shines through on every page, the practical advice constantly framed by illustrative stories of survival and endurance. It was principally written for distribution to Merchant Marine crews, who stood a high chance of being torpedoed or otherwise sunk during their operations. Should the worst happen, the odds of staying alive were not good. Only about 50 per cent of sailors aboard a sunken ship survived; in very cold climates, such as the North Atlantic or the Arctic waters, the chances dropped to 1 in 100. Manual advice such as *How to Abandon Ship* were not guarantees of survival, but if followed to the letter could dramatically tilt the odds in your favour.

How to Abandon Ship (1943)

2. Abandon Ship

Do not rush. Sudden sinkings have been rare. But casualties brought about by panicked men dashing needlessly into peril have been frequent. Fourteen men were saved out of the torpedoed *Naco*'s crew of 42. Walter Swank reported: "The men who kept cool and used their heads were those who managed to be saved."

If Ernest Cartwright, one of the three survivors of a freighter shelled more than fifty times, had rushed to get into the port lifeboat, he would have lived less than two minutes. Before they could reach the water, the men in that boat were killed by shellfire. With no alternative, Cartwright dived overboard. In the waterborne starboard lifeboat he found six more shipmates, four of them dead. These men had rushed to their death. They had been unable to pause long enough to choose the lesser risk, which was to remain aboard. The freighter itself did not sink for two hours — long after the U-boat had ceased firing.

The chief mate of a torpedoed Panamanian freighter, Hawkins Fudske, entered a lifeboat too soon and was killed by an exploding shell. Yet the men were able to reboard their ship the next day and take her into Mobile, Alabama.

Captain Frank C. Girardeau and all but nine of his men were able to reboard their abandoned ship, after a night spent in the lifeboats, and have her towed into port.

Suction. — A slowly sinking vessel may submerge without creating a suction. Vincent Halli- burton, from the torpedoed *Ceiba*, reported: "While standing on the boat deck, I felt the ship disappear from under my feet. I started to swim and I picked up a raft." Few men caught within the suction area of a swiftly sinking ship, except those wearing life suits, have survived.

Hans Sundby, carpenter from the torpedoed Norwegian freighter *Erviken*, reported: "I had the guy to the davit across my shoulders and this prevented me from swimming and caused me to follow the vessel downwards. When I got so far down that I found a terrific pressure against my head, especially the ears, I got free from the wire. I shot up with tremendous power. The suit saved my life by bringing me so quickly to the surface on account of the air trapped inside it."

Man Overboard. — Do not jump into the water. Unless, like Ernest Cartwright, you have no alternative, or you have to do so to reach a liferaft. If you are wearing a lifejacket containing cork, you are in danger of breaking a rib or your collar bone.

A seaman jumped overboard from the freighter on which Fudske lost his life, and was killed by a shark, though the vessel reached port with forty-two men.

Fidley Grating. — A man aboard the torpedoed *Collamer*, on watch below, lost his life because of a permanent grating on the fidley skylight.

Engine Room Ladders. — Rudolph C. Welmann, second assistant, suggested: "Rope lad-ders should be hung in the engine room and fire-room so that men will know their location and be able to escape if the regular ladders are blown away."

Emergency Escapes. — Thoroughly acquaint yourself with the emergency escapes. Four men on the *Prusa* were lost because they forgot about the emergency escape through the steering engine room. A steam line was severed in the regular passage, making it impossible to leave that way. Yet these men, who were seen in the quarters alive and apparently uninjured after the explosion, had only to go through the steering engine room up through a manhole onto the poop deck, as two other men did.

Brattice Cloth. — For years brattice cloth – non-inflammable – has been used by miners to shut off a tunnel in the case of fire or a drift when about to shoot a heading. It is now being purchased for many ships, and is of service in partitioning off open alleyways to prevent the passage of flame.

Discuss the feasibility of making a large windsail of brattice cloth to surround the Jacob's ladder leading up from the engine room to the skylight.

Life Suit. — Hans Sundby of the *Erviken* reported: "The engineers at work had made the mistake of having their suits in their cabins instead of the passage to the engine room."

Seaworthiness. — Be sure your lifeboat is seaworthy. This may seem needless advice. Yet in the past bottoms have come out of many lifeboats. One lifeboat of a United Nations freighter, torpedoed 200 miles from Bermuda, leaked so badly that for eleven days the men were unable to stop bailing.

Equipment. — Do not take it for granted that all the equipment required by law is in your lifeboat. Norman Leo Sampson, the third assistant of a torpedoed freighter, reported that nine of his shipmates were trapped in a lifeboat with no oars. The boat drifted into a sea of blazing oil.

Whistle. — Every man should have a whistle made fast around his neck, so that if he is in the water, he can blow the whistle to draw attention.

A severely burned British seaman from a torpedoed gasoline tanker was on the keel of an overturned lifeboat for five days. He was washed off five times, chiefly at night. Since he had a whistle, his shipmates were able to locate him, otherwise he would have been lost.

Life Light. — Life lights are manufactured for both jackets and life rings. With good visibility these lights will provide a possibility of attracting rescuers within a radius of at least four miles. Within the visibility range of shore, they offer a three-way chance of drawing attention – from land, sea, and air.

Abandon-Ship Package. — If you are on watch, you should have your life suit, extra clothes, and abandon-ship package with you, so you will not have to lose time returning to your quarters.

Wire Basket. — Have the ship's wire baskets or stretchers easily accessible, so that injured persons may be lowered to a waterborne lifeboat. A wire basket may save a simple break from becoming a compound fracture, with its resultant gangrene and possible death.

Papers. — After signing the ship's articles, place your papers and valuables in a deposit box ashore. This will relieve your mind of any concern for their safety.

The officers should leave their licenses remaining in the frames aboard ship.

Clothes. — Do not sleep undressed. Vincent Santiago, A. B. aboard the *Leslie*, slept almost the entire trip with his clothes on. The first night he took his clothes off, the Leslie was torpedoed. For three months McPherson, second mate of the *Exminster*, wore his clothes to bed. The first night he donned pajamas, the *Exminster* was torpedoed.

Even in the tropics have cold-weather clothes in your abandon-ship package, or ready to put on without delay. During five hours of drifting, eleven men clinging to liferafts from the stricken U.S. destroyer *Jacob Jones* succumbed to the cold and slipped into the sea. Yet George Pantall and Thomas Ryan Moody survived. They each had the judgment to don three extra suits of heavy winter underwear.

When a tanker, of which Captain Theron P. Davenport was the master, was torpedoed off the coast of Georgia early in April, the crew had ample time to gather their gear before abandoning ship. Yet most of the men neglected to take along sufficient clothing. Consequently, during the ten hours they were adrift, many of them were severely and needlessly sunburned.

Oilskins. — Two men, at least, should bring along oilskins. They will be of vital use to the men on watch.

Extra Food. — You should provide a means to open the potato locker quickly. Get a sack of potatoes in your lifeboat, and a sack of onions, if possible, or turnips. Because of their high water content, these vegetables will serve a double purpose in your rations. Canned tomatoes are important. Do not pass up the bottles of jam. The sugar in them will provide energy.

Emergency provisions should be stored in many small watertight containers rather than in one large one. This will lessen the chance of losing your supplies through a container being punctured by shot and the contents being destroyed by salt water.

Other Equipment. —

Jackknife. Do not neglect to take along a knife.

Flashlight. If you have a flashlight and batteries, take them with you. The *Robin Moor*'s boat had four torches, in addition to the one required by law.

Rosendo Ramos from the torpedoed *Republic*, reported: "If each man had a flashlight for use after the lights went out, he could probably have found other ways of escape after the ladder was broken."

Mason Jar. A Mason jar will keep your matches and other small items dry.

Toilet Paper. Take a roll with you.

Flare Pistol. Be sure your lifeboat is equipped with a flare pistol.

Rockets. If time permits, get two or three of the rockets which are stowed on the bridge.

Plug. — So no one will have difficulty finding the plug, mark it — plug. Paint an arrow in white pointing to it.

Greenwich Time. — If possible, set your watch to Greenwich time. The mate in your boat may not have a chance to set his watch. He will not be able to calculate longitude with any accuracy without Greenwich time when taking sights.

Orders. — Get your orders from the mate. But if you are on your own, be sure to get one boat into the water. That can take care of a reighter's whole crew.

Panic. — Night puts an added burden on you and you must take extra precautions, because at night there is sure to be more panic than in the daytime.

Time. — The experience of B. A. Baker, the *Prusa*'s third mate, will give you a gauge by which you can judge your own time in an emergency. After she was torpedoed, the *Prusa* sank in exactly nine minutes. Baker was asleep when the torpedo hit. He went to the bridge and got his sextant, chronometer, and navigation books. He stowed them in the boat and helped lower the boat. Then he went back and tried to get the radio operator to leave. Returning to his room, he obtained a sweater, and then jumped overboard. He swam about 200 feet to the lifeboat. The *Prusa* sank as he was being pulled into the boat.

Self-Control. — If you find yourself being overcome by weakness – having "butterflies in your stomach" – sit down or crouch for a few moments. This is almost a sure-fire method to aid you in getting control of yourself.

Bullet-Hole Plugs. — Each lifeboat is supplied with bullet-hole plugs, but stove bolts and nuts, used with candlewicking, also serve the purpose. Take along a bundle of rags to be used with the plugs.

Alcohol Burner. — Take along some canned heat. Then if your water supply becomes frozen, you can thaw it out.

Salt-Water Soap. — Take along a bar of salt-water soap.

Life Preserver. — If you are wearing a heavy coat, do not put a life preserver on over it. Put the preserver on under the coat. Then, if necessary, you can slip the coat off, and still have the protection of the preserver.

The US tanker *Dixie Arrow* burns and sinks after being torpedoed off Cape Hatteras by *U-71* on 26 March 1942.

3. Buoyancy

Do not jump overboard unless you have no alternative. That is what this explanation of buoyancy — the power to keep afloat — is intended to impress upon you.

For a vessel to stay afloat, the upward pressure of the water must be equal to the downward pressure or weight of the vessel. However, because a ship is torpedoed, it does not necessarily follow that the balance of opposing pressures is going to be so altered that the ship must sink. Four men on the torpedoed tanker *Malay* were unable to consider this, and they lost their lives, though the *Malay* itself made port safely.

A vessel is composed of several units. Each hold, as well as the fireroom and engine room, is an independent buoyant section.

Picture in your mind a small freight vessel. Visualize each hold as being detached from the other. Each, as you picture it, is now floating independently. The engine room and fireroom, you will see, are floating deep. The #1 and #4 holds are not quite so deep. The #3 hold has less draft, while the #2 hold has the least depth of all. The sums of all these individual buoyancies make the total buoyancy of the vessel.

Though the tanker *E. H. Blum* was broken in two by a torpedo, the forward half still had sufficient buoyancy to permit it to be towed to port. Captain Theodore Bockhoff understood the buoyancy set-up of his stricken freighter after it was hit by a torpedo. That is why he ordered Seaman James Sherlock, who was running for the starboard boat, to wait. A few moments later, as the starboard lifeboat reached the water with six men in it, a second torpedo blew it to bits.

When the torpedoed tanker *Gulf* trade broke in two, nine men were on the stern. Seaman Leonard Smith wanted to jump overboard. Guy F. Chadwick, the chief engineer, reminded Smith that the water was cold. "Let's stick with the ship," Chadwick advised, "as long as she'll stick with us." At the very least, the chief's understanding of buoyancy spared a man from exposure and frostbite.

Suppose the vessel is loaded with lumber, and a hold is stove in. Since the specific gravity of wood runs from one-fifth to a slight fraction beyond that of water, the only loss is in the reserve buoyancy, as the lumber's buoyant qualities will substitute for the loss of actual buoyancy. The space which the sea can occupy is only the area not already taken up by the lumber.

Often, when only one or two buoyant sections are immediately damaged, the vessel eventually sinks. The *China Arrow*, torpedoed twice, took an hour to sink. This was probably due to the fact that while the destruction of tanks in the vicinity of the blasts was not enough to sink the *China Arrow*, the detonations sheared plates and loosened rivets in the tanks beyond. Buoyancy is often lost on tankers when heat from the oil blaze buckles the plates. Our point is that it takes time for this buoyancy to be lost.

This is borne out by the Latvian freighter *Ciltvaira*. After abandoning ship the men were able to go back, run up SOS flags, and salvage valuables. Captain T. R. Hennevig returned to his crippled freighter eight hours after it had been torpedoed and shelled. A sugar transport vessel, torpedoed off Nuevitas, Cuba, remained afloat and was beached, though 22 crewmen died when lifeboats were sunk by gunfire.

A hold stowed with general cargo presents a serious condition. All the buoyancy of that hold would be lost. Grain cargo likewise adds a threat to a stricken vessel. Expanding from absorbed water, the grain will exert pressure on the watertight bulkhead and loosen rivets.

In short, experience and the laws of physics indicate that men usually have more time to abandon ship than they allow themselves. However, statistics are often contradicted by an individual situation, so don't let them lull you into carelessness. Ships have sunk in five minutes or less.

For your protection discuss with the mates and engineers the buoyancy problems of your ship. And before you jump, remember that Bryan Lloyd, a seaman, had time to swim back to his ship from a swamped lifeboat, rest five minutes, and release a liferaft. Captain Knut O. Bringedal was able to return to his torpedoed vessel three times. And the tanker *Esso Bolivar*, with water ballast, was towed into port with a 40-foot hole blasted in her side.

[. . .]

6. Waterborne

Once your highly buoyant lifeboat is waterborne, no difficult process is required to keep it from capsizing. You merely must have the weight distributed properly. Allow no one to stand on a thwart. Five men can do all that is necessary to get the boat away from the ship's side. In a heavy sea maintain a low center of gravity by having the balance of the crew keep down on the bottom boards.

Blocks. — As soon as the releasing gear is operated, watch out for swinging blocks.

Falls. — Falls may be used to slide down in abandoning ship.

Boat Hook. — Have a man shove off from the ship's side with a boat hook or oar.

Painter. — Have the bow man haul as much of the painter into the boat as possible before he cuts loose. This will give you extra line. Pulling up on the rope will put the boat in motion, enabling the man at the tiller to steer, providing the sea is not too rough.

Oar Lashings. — When letting go the lashings on the oars, be sure only half of them are turned loose. Otherwise, if the boat capsizes, all the oars will be lost.

Oarsmen. — It is not necessary to man all of the oars. One oarsman on each side will be able to get the boat away from the ship quickly. They should row immediately at right angles to the ship, to eliminate the possibility of another boat being lowered on top of the waterborne one.

Rowing. — It is difficult to row in a heavy sea. The men can last at it about fifteen minutes, and by making every stroke count, can perhaps get a half mile from the ship.

Be sure you do not start pulling on the oar before it is in the water.

Keep your eye on the stroke oar on each side of the boat.

Put the weight of your body on the oar. In a boat properly rowed a thrumming noise issues from the oars and gives a sense of timing.

In a double-banked boat be careful that you do not draw a longer stroke than the man in front of you. If you do, you are liable to dig him in the back with the handle of your oar.

Feathering. — While it is the customary practice to grasp the handle of the oar with both hands on the upper side, many oarsmen find it easier to feather with one hand on the upper side and one hand on the underside. This is the grip used by seamen of the West Indies. They are exceptional oarsmen. The grip is also used by the Ellis and Gilbert Islanders, and no finer oarsmen live.

Do not feather until the blade is clear of the water. If you do so, the oar will be forced down by the way of the boat and it will likely foul the oar behind you.

At this time feathering is not important. Your chief concern should be to get clear of the ship's suction area.

Life Preserver. — If everything is behaving properly, and the men realize the importance of keeping the weight distributed evenly, there is no need to continue wearing your life preserver. Drop it to the bottom of the boat.

Sea Anchor. — Put out the sea anchor and rest up. Do not attempt to set sail immediately. Wait until shock, confusion, and panic have subsided. When the panicked crew of the torpedoed Norwegian freighter *Blink* tried to hoist a sail, the lifeboat capsized, throwing 23 men into icy water and immediately costing one man's life. Food, water, oars, and sail were lost.

Man Overboard. — Be sure no one is near a churning propeller. Herbert L. Gardner, Jr., wiper from an Atlantic Refining Co. tanker, saw two shipmates caught in the propeller's suction and dragged into the blades to their death.

Men have died by being struck by rescue boats. Approach a man in the water no closer than the distance needed to reach him with an out-stretched oar.

Pistol. — Be sure that no hot-headed shipmate has a gun. Firing it at the sub will only draw fire on your boat. Besides, it is unlawful for merchant seamen to possess firearms.

Panic. — Away from the ship in a lifeboat that is riding nicely, you have little or no cause for panic. When the *Robin Moor* men heard machine-gun fire, they were stricken with terror that they would be shot. But the sub's gunners were merely indulging in target practice, firing at wreckage.

If the enemy intended to machine-gun a crew, they generally would not let the crew get off the ship.

The sub commander who sank the *Robin Moor* provided extra rations for the crew and first-aid materials for Chief Officer Mundy. P. H. Janssen, fireman from a torpedoed American freighter, after being hauled aboard a submarine by the German crew, spent five minutes on its deck before he was transferred to a lifeboat.

More likely than not, you will find that enemy sailors will give you the same treatment they would expect to receive.

Bullet Hole. — Do not give up because a hole is shot in your boat. The airtanks will float her, and with proper tools any boat can be patched at sea.

In a sheet-metal boat, if you have sheet-metal screws, a prick punch and a screwdriver, by cutting up an airtank you can patch in an hour a hole one foot in diameter.

F. J. Mills, chief engineer, patched a damaged lifeboat with a piece of canvas. His shipmates held him under water, while he tacked the canvas in place, coming up at intervals for air.

Strain on Painter. — Do not unhook the forward fall until a strain is on the painter. If the releasing gear is operated before the painter is taut, the boat may come up with a violent jerk.

Lifeline. — Never use a lifeline as a painter. A turn taken with a lifeline around a thwart capsized a lifeboat, drowning several men.

Burning Oil. — Many lifeboats have been rowed through oil flames, so do not jump over- board if your boat is surrounded by fire. Row against the wind to avoid gases as well as fire.

In carrying out rowing orders remember that you are facing the stern. Port will be on your right, starboard on your left.

Overturned Lifeboat. — A capsized lifeboat can be righted by the combined weight of four or five men on one side.

SOURCES

CHAPTER 1

Booth, Lieutenant-Commander E. C. Talbot, *His Majesty's Merchant Navy* (Sampson Low, Marston & Co. Ltd, 1940)

United States Maritime Service Training Manual, Deck Branch Training (War Shipping Administration Training Organization, 1943)

CHAPTER 2

Booth, Lieutenant-Commander E. C. Talbot, *His Majesty's Merchant Navy* (Sampson Low, Marston & Co. Ltd, 1940)

General Instructions for Commanding Officers of Naval Armed Guards on Merchant Ships (Navy Department, 1944)

CHAPTER 3

Admiralty Merchant-Ship Defence Instructions (AMDI) (Admiralty, May 1944), accessed National Archives, ADM 199/2368

United States Maritime Service Training Manual: Deck Branch Training (War Shipping Administration Training Organization, 1943)

CHAPTER 4

King's Regulations & Admiralty Instructions (HMSO, 1913)

Booth, Lieutenant-Commander E. C. Talbot, *His Majesty's Merchant Navy* (Sampson Low, Marston & Co. Ltd, 1940)

Organisation and Conduct of British Convoys (Admiralty, c. 1941), accessed National Archives, ADM 199/5

Lecture on Visual Signalling for Officers of the Merchant Navy (H.M. Signal School, 1937)

CHAPTER 5

Richards, Phil and John J. Branigan, *How to Abandon Ship*, Cornell Maritime Press (1943)
Safety for Seamen, Medical Division, War Shipping Administration-United Seaman's Service
    (*c.* 1943)

GÉRARD DE VILLIERS

SAS LA SÉRIE CULTE ENFIN ADAPTÉE EN BD !

SAS Tome 1 PACTE AVEC LE DIABLE | DÉJÀ PARU

GÉRARD DE VILLIERS

SAS LA SÉRIE CULTE ENFIN ADAPTÉE EN BD !

NOUVEAUTÉ RTL 9

LYCOS.fr

SAS Tome 2 LE SABRE DE BIN-LADEN | PARUTION 24 OCTOBRE 2006